GASES, LIQUIDS, AND SOLIDS

Grolier Educational
SHERMAN TURNPIKE, DANBURY, CONNECTICUT 06816

First published in the United States in 1998
by Grolier Educational, Sherman Turnpike,
Danbury, CT 06816

Author
Brian Knapp, BSc, PhD
Project consultant
*Keith B. Walshaw, MA, BSc, DPhil
(Head of Chemistry, Leighton Park School)*
Project Director
Duncan McCrae, BSc
Editor
Mary Sanders, BSc
Special photography
Ian Gledhill
**Electronic page makeup
and illustrations**
The Ascenders Partnership
Designed and produced by
EARTHSCAPE EDITIONS
Print consultants
Chromo Litho Ltd
Reproduced in Malaysia by
Global Colour
Printed and bound in Italy by
L.E.G.O. SpA

Library of Congress Cataloging-in-Publication Data
ChemLab
    p. cm.
    Includes indexes.
    Contents: v.1.Gases, liquids, and solids –
v.2.Elements, compounds, and mixtures – v.3.The
periodic table – v.4.Metals – v.5.Acids, bases, and salts
– v.6.Heat and combustion – v.7.Oxidation and
reduction – v.8.Air and water chemistry – v.9.Carbon
chemistry – v.10.Energy and chemical change –
v.11.Preparations – v.12. Tests.
    ISBN 0–7172–9146–4 (set). – ISBN 0–7172–9147–2 (v.1).
    1. Chemistry – Juvenile literature. [1. Chemistry.]
I. Grolier Educational (Firm)
QD35.C52 1997
540–dc21   97–23250
                                                          CIP
                                                          AC

Picture credits
All photographs are from the **Earthscape
Editions** photolibrary except the following:
(c=center t=top b=bottom l=left r=right)
Mary Evans Picture Library 8tc

*This product is manufactured from sustainable
managed forests. For every tree cut down at least one
more is planted.*

Contents

HOW TO USE THIS BOOK
These two pages show you how to get the most from this book.

❶ THE CONTENTS

Use the table of contents to see how this book is divided into themes. Each theme may have one or more demonstrations.

❷ THEMES

Each theme begins with a theory section on yellow-colored paper. Major themes may contain several pages of theory for the demonstrations that are presented on the subsequent pages. They also contain biographies of scientists whose work was important in the understanding of the theme.

❸ DEMONSTRATIONS

Demonstrations are at the heart of any chemistry study. However, many demonstrations cannot easily be shown to a whole class for health and safety reasons, because the demonstration requires a closeup view, because it is over too quickly, takes too long to complete, or because it requires special apparatus. The demonstrations shown here have been photographed especially to overcome these problems and give you a very closeup view of the key stages in each reaction.

The text, pictures, and diagrams are closely connected. To get the best from the demonstration, look closely at each picture as soon as its reference occurs in the text.

Many of the pictures show enlarged views of parts of the demonstration to help you see exactly what is happening. Notice, too, that most pictures form part of a sequence. You will find that it pays to look at the picture sequence more than once, and always be careful to make sure you can see exactly what is described in any picture before you move on.

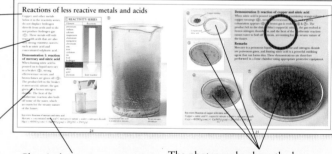

The main heading for a demonstration or a set of demonstrations.

An introduction expands on the heading, summarizing the demonstration or group of demonstrations and their context in the theme.

Each demonstration is carefully explained and illustrated with photographs and, where necessary, with diagrams, tables, and graphs. The illustrations referred to are numbered ①, ②, ③, etc.

Chemical equations are shown where appropriate (see the explanation of equations at the bottom of page 5).

The photographs show the key stages that you might see if witnessing a demonstration firsthand. Examine them very carefully against the text description.

APPARATUS

The demonstrations have been carefully conducted as representative examples of the main chemical processes. The apparatus used is standard; but other choices are possible, and you may see different equipment in your laboratory. So make sure you understand the principles behind the apparatus selected. The key pieces of apparatus are defined in the glossary.

❹ GLOSSARY OF TECHNICAL TERMS

Words with which you may be unfamiliar are shown in small capitals where they first occur in the text. Use the glossary on pages 66–74 to find more information about these technical words. Over four hundred items are presented alphabetically.

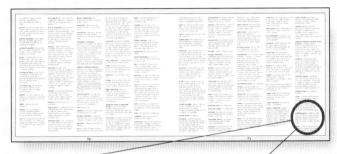

oxidizing agent: a substance that removes electrons from another substance being oxidized (and therefore is itself reduced) in a redox reaction. *Example:* chlorine (Cl_2).

❺ INDEX TO ALL VOLUMES IN THE SET

To look for key words in any of the 12 volumes that make up the ChemLab set, use the Master Index on pages 75 to 80. The instructions on page 75 show you how to cross-reference between volumes.

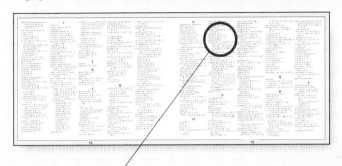

The most important locations of the term "oxidizing agent" are given in a master index that includes references to all of the volumes in the ChemLab set.

ABBREVIATIONS

Units are in the international metric system. Some units of measurement are abbreviated, or shortened, as follows:
°C = degrees Celsius
km = kilometer
m = meter
cm = centimeter
mm = millimeter
sq m = square meter
g = gram
kg = kilogram
kJ = kilojoule
l = liter

❻ CHEMICAL EQUATIONS

Important or relevant chemical equations are shown in written and symbolic form along with additional information.

What the reaction equation illustrates

Word equation

Symbol equation
The symbols for each element can be found in any Periodic Table.

Where relevant, the oxidation state is shown as Roman numerals in parentheses.

The symbol indicating the state of each substance is shown as follows:
(s) = solid
(g) = gaseous
(l) = liquid
(aq) = aqueous
(conc) = concentrated

EQUATION: Reaction of copper and nitric acid

Copper + nitric acid ⇨ *copper(II) nitrate + water + nitrogen dioxide*

$Cu(s) + 4HNO_3(conc) \Rightarrow Cu(NO_3)_2(aq) + 2H_2O(l) + 2NO_2(g)$
Blue

The two halves of the chemical equation are separated by the arrow that shows the progression of the reaction. Each side of the equation must balance.

Sometimes additional descriptions are given below the symbol equation.

The correct number of atoms, ions, and molecules and their proportions in any compound are shown by the numbers. A free electron is shown as an e⁻.

STATES OF MATTER

Matter normally exists in one of three arrangements, known as states — as a SOLID, LIQUID, or GAS (①). A substance can be changed from one state into another simply by changing the temperature. For example, when liquid water exceeds its BOILING POINT, it becomes a gas as steam or water vapor. When water falls below its FREEZING POINT, it becomes the solid we call ice. Of course, water will also change between liquid and gas at temperatures lower than the boiling point, a process known as EVAPORATION, and it can also change from gas to liquid below the boiling point, a process called CONDENSATION. Water can also change from being a solid to a gas, or even from a gas to a solid, without becoming a liquid in-between, and this change is known as SUBLIMATION. But, whichever state it is in, matter remains chemically the same.

Gases are the least dense form of matter. They are made of MOLECULES that are free to move about. This means that they exert uniform PRESSURE in all directions, and having no shape themselves, they can take the shape and volume of whatever container they are placed in (②) (also see page 12). Gases can be compressed.

Liquids are midway between solids and gases. Liquids have no shape and tend to flow and fill the lowest part of any container and to take the container's shape (③). Although the particles (ATOMS, IONS, or molecules) that make up a liquid are free to move around,

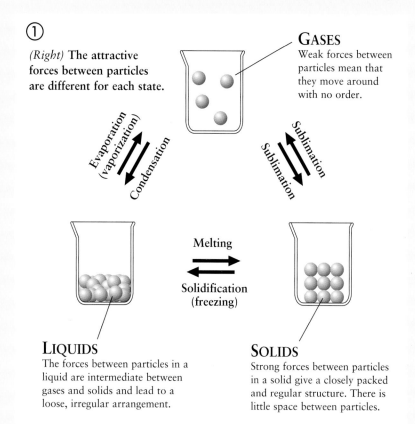

① *(Right)* **The attractive forces between particles are different for each state.**

GASES
Weak forces between particles mean that they move around with no order.

Evaporation (vaporization)

Condensation

Sublimation

Sublimation

Melting

Solidification (freezing)

LIQUIDS
The forces between particles in a liquid are intermediate between gases and solids and lead to a loose, irregular arrangement.

SOLIDS
Strong forces between particles in a solid give a closely packed and regular structure. There is little space between particles.

Gases, such as this brown bromine, will rapidly expand to occupy the whole shape of the container they are in.

they remain in contact with each other, and a liquid does not change its volume.

Both gases and liquids are grouped as FLUIDS, that is, they are mobile forms of matter.

A solid is a form of matter that has a relatively fixed shape that is not easy to change ((④)). Thus, for example, a piece of steel only changes shape when a large force is applied, such as comes from a hammer blow. Most solids are composed of regularly arranged particles (atoms, ions, or molecules) as CRYSTALS (also see page 17).

The history of ideas about matter

Since ancient times many scientists believed that any solid object could be divided up into smaller and smaller pieces. The ancient Greeks had developed the idea that solid matter is made up of tiny building blocks and had given such tiny pieces the name "atom" (from the Greek *atomos*, meaning "indivisible"). By the end of the 17th century Isaac Newton had described the quantity of matter as MASS, and he had explained that gravity gives matter its WEIGHT.

It is now known that an atom is the simplest unit of an ELEMENT (for example, oxygen, O) that can combine with the simplest units of other elements (such as hydrogen, H) to create a molecule of a COMPOUND, such as water (H_2O). Thus atoms are the smallest form of an element; molecules are the smallest particles that still possess the characteristics of a compound. Compounds always consist of more than one kind of atom.

③

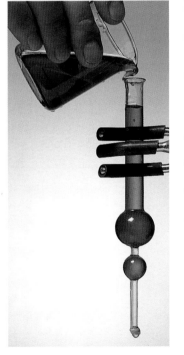

Liquids will occupy the shape of the part of the container they are in.

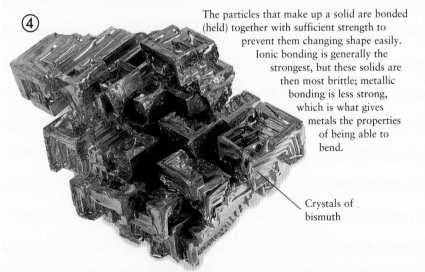
④

The particles that make up a solid are bonded (held) together with sufficient strength to prevent them changing shape easily. Ionic bonding is generally the strongest, but these solids are then most brittle; metallic bonding is less strong, which is what gives metals the properties of being able to bend.

Crystals of bismuth

Antoine Laurent Lavoisier

Antoine Lavoisier (1743–1794) was born in Paris, the son of a prosperous lawyer. He was interested in geology, and to learn about minerals he attended chemistry classes and soon became interested in a wide range of science. His earliest research led to publications on the chemical nature of gypsum (1765), a study of ways to improve the street lighting of Paris, and on mineral waters. He was elected to the Royal Academy of Sciences in Paris in 1768.

In 1775 Lavoisier was appointed to the National Gunpowder Commission. He lived in the Paris Arsenal, where he established a fine laboratory for his scientific work.

Lavoisier has been called the father of chemistry. Although the major classes of chemicals – acids, alkalis, salts, alkaline earths, and metals — had already been decided by Lavoisier's time, gases were poorly known, and many chemical reactions were explained by the strange theory of a fire-matter called phlogiston. Lavoisier's main contribution was to begin to develop a logical theory to pull all these parts of chemistry together. His insistence on the need to make careful measurements was particularly valuable, and from this came the recognition that the weight of the reactants must equal the products of a reaction.

Lavoisier was the first scientist to explain that any substance can exist in three states: gas, liquid, and solid. The key to these changes of state was seen to be associated with heat, and for this he used the term caloric.

Lavoisier was caught up in the French Revolution, and he was imprisoned and finally guillotined based on trumped up charges. At the time a fellow scientist remarked: "It took only an instant to cut off that head, and a hundred years may not produce another like it."

Bonding

The building blocks of all matter are atoms. Atoms may become charged, in which case they are ions. However, to build with atoms or ions there have to be mechanisms to bind atoms together, the equivalent of the cement needed to build a wall with building blocks. This atomic cement comes in many forms, and the nature of each form determines the nature of matter.

Solids, liquids, and gases are all composed of particles. The forces attracting the particles to each other determine the properties of the material. The various types of such bonds are described below.

Covalent bonding

Covalent bonding occurs when atoms join together by sharing ELECTRONS. Many nonmetal atoms bond in this way, for example, hydrogen atoms bond covalently to make the molecule hydrogen (H_2). By sharing electrons, the outer shell of each hydrogen atom (which has only one electron) becomes full (it has two electrons) and so is stable. The same is the case for chlorine (⑤) (in this case chlorine has 7 electrons in its outer sheell, but it become stable when it has 8 electrons in the outer shell).

Covalent bonding can also occur in compounds. For example, water is made of two atoms of hydrogen covalently bonded to one atom of oxygen to make the water molecule (H_2O); methane gas (CH_4) is made of a carbon atom covalently bonded to four hydrogen atoms.

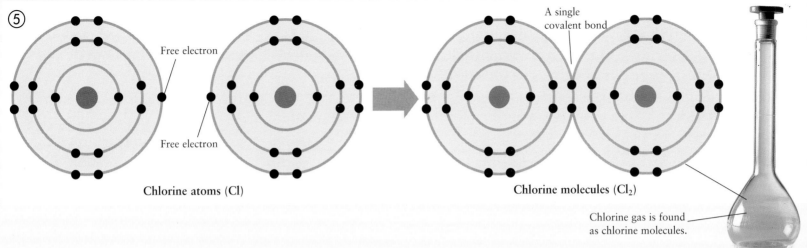

⑤

Free electron

Free electron

Chlorine atoms (Cl)

A single covalent bond

Chlorine molecules (Cl₂)

Chlorine gas is found as chlorine molecules.

Covalent bonding produces small, easily separated, molecules. This is why substances that are gases are covalently bonded. Liquids or solids with low melting and boiling points are also likely to be covalent. Most covalently bonded molecules are also SOLUBLE in ORGANIC SOLVENTS but are generally insoluble in water (although common exceptions include oxygen, chlorine, ammonia, sugar, and alcohol).

Metallic bonding

A metal is made of closely packed, positive ions (CATIONS) embedded in a "sea" of electrons that bond the ions together (⑥). Every ion is surrounded by six others to produce a hexagonal pattern of packing, and this gives metals their high densities. The strong bonds between the ions and the free electrons are responsible for the high melting points of metals and for them being good conductors of heat and electricity.

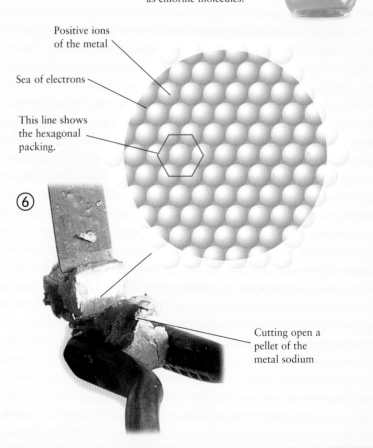

Positive ions of the metal

Sea of electrons

This line shows the hexagonal packing.

⑥

Cutting open a pellet of the metal sodium

Ionic bonding

In compounds containing ionic bonds one atom transfers one or more electrons from its outer shell to another atom. This occurs most readily with very reactive nonmetal elements (such as oxygen and chlorine) and with the most reactive metals (such as sodium).

When this transfer of electrons occurs, the atoms change from being electrically neutral to charged ions. One ion becomes positively charged, the other negatively charged (an ANION). The oppositely charged ions are attracted to one another, and they form an ionic bond.

Sodium chloride is an ionic compound. Each sodium atom gives up the only electron it has in its outer shell to a neighboring chlorine atom, which has only one electron missing from its outer shell. In this way an ionic bond is formed (⑦). At the same time, both the sodium and the chlorine become more stable ions.

Because like charges repel and unlike charges attract, ionic bonding results in a regular pattern of ions (⑧). Also, because the oppositely charged ions attract one another equally in every direction, they do not form small simple pairs or groups but grow up into crystals of ever-increasing size (⑨).

Ionic bonds are very strong, and most solids with ionic bonding have high melting points because a large amount of (heat) energy is needed to break their bonds.

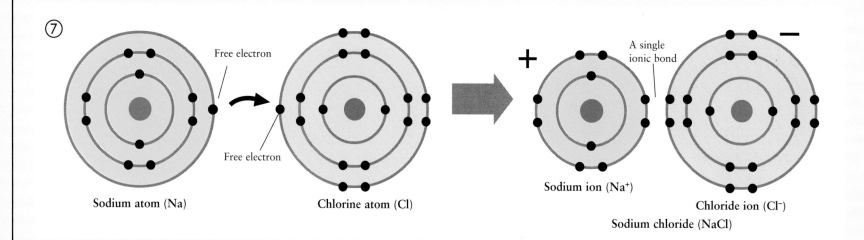

⑦

Free electron

Free electron

Sodium atom (Na)   Chlorine atom (Cl)

+

A single ionic bond

−

Sodium ion (Na⁺)

Chloride ion (Cl⁻)

Sodium chloride (NaCl)

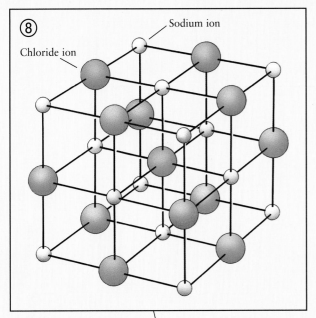

⑧

Chloride ion

Sodium ion

(Above) **This diagram represents the structure of solid sodium chloride. The lines between the sodium and chloride ions represent the ionic bonds.**

(Right) **The seven crystal systems to which all crystals belong.**

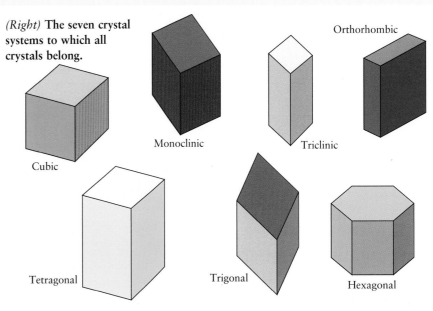

Cubic

Monoclinic

Triclinic

Orthorhombic

Tetragonal

Trigonal

Hexagonal

(Below) **The crystals of sodium chloride (common salt) are cubic, and because the sodium and chloride ions are held together by ionic bonds, sodium chloride is an ionic compound.**

⑨

(Left) **Hexagonal structure of beryl. Beryl is an ionic compound.**

(Right) **Rhombohedral (orthorhombic) structure of calcite. Calcite is an ionic compound.**

11

Observing the relative density of gases

The molecules of a gas are free to move about and have no shape of their own, expanding to fill a space.

Gases prepared in the laboratory can be contained as bubbles in a film of liquid.

This simple technique allows the DENSITY of different gases to be compared with that of air.

Each molecule of gas has a density that reflects the atomic mass of the elements from which it is made. So, at normal air pressure hydrogen is lighter than air, whereas carbon dioxide is heavier.

Demonstration 1: preparing bubbles of hydrogen

Hydrogen has an atomic mass of one and is the lightest chemical ELEMENT known. It has one-twelfth of the density of air. It is found as pairs of atoms, covalently bonded as molecules (H_2) (see page 8).

Hydrogen is prepared by reacting dilute hydrochloric acid from a dropper funnel with zinc granules in a flask (①). The gas evolved is connected to a clay pipe. The clay pipe is a convenient piece of improvised apparatus, across which a detergent film can be drawn and a bubble created. The detergent film is obtained by dipping the mouth of the clay pipe in a bowl of detergent.

It is important to flush the air from the apparatus. Air-filled bubbles (air and liquid bubble mixture) are slightly more dense than air, and so

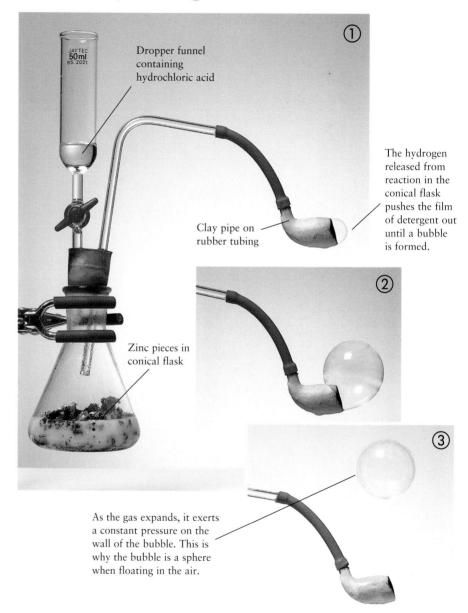

① Dropper funnel containing hydrochloric acid

JAY TEC 50ml BS 2021

The hydrogen released from reaction in the conical flask pushes the film of detergent out until a bubble is formed.

Clay pipe on rubber tubing

Zinc pieces in conical flask

②

③

As the gas expands, it exerts a constant pressure on the wall of the bubble. This is why the bubble is a sphere when floating in the air.

such bubbles sink gently after they have left the pipe. Each time a bubble has left the pipe, the pipe mouth must be inverted into the bubble mixture so that a new film can be created. Soon, it is quite clear that the bubbles are filling with a gas that is less dense than air because the bubbles are straining to rise from the top of the pipe (②). When they finally break loose, the hydrogen-filled bubbles rise quickly through the air before they burst (③).

Demonstration 2: preparing bubbles of carbon dioxide

Each carbon dioxide molecule has a total MOLECULAR MASS of about 44 and is nearly twice as dense as air. The molecules are composed of three atoms covalently bonded to one another (CO_2).

This demonstration uses the same apparatus as for preparation of hydrogen, but in this case dilute hydrochloric acid is dripped onto calcium carbonate to generate carbon dioxide gas (④). Again, the first bubbles will mainly be filled with air, but soon bubbles are generated that sag dramatically from the pipe (⑤) and then sink quickly after they have left the pipe bowl (⑥).

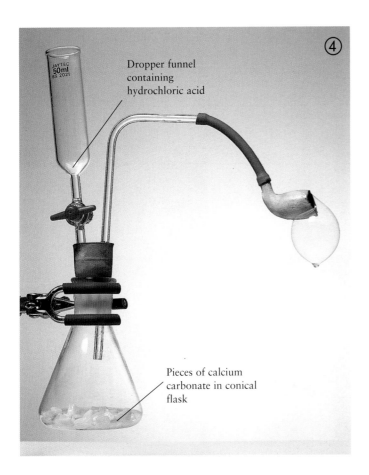

④

Dropper funnel containing hydrochloric acid

Pieces of calcium carbonate in conical flask

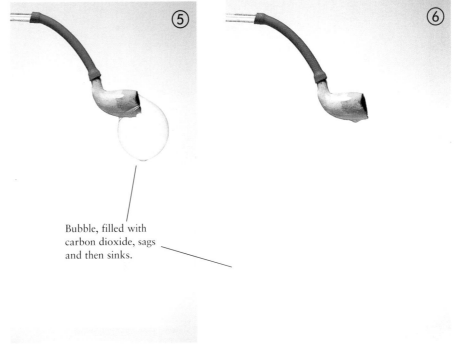

⑤

⑥

Bubble, filled with carbon dioxide, sags and then sinks.

Growing crystals from a supersaturated solution

The process by which a solid (solute) comes out of a solution is known as crystallization. For crystallization to occur, the solution must be supersaturated (see the description in the box on the right).

Demonstration 1: preparing a dilute solution of copper(II) sulfate

A copper(II) sulfate solution is prepared by reacting copper(II) oxide (copper(II) carbonate can be used) with warm, dilute sulfuric acid (①). The solution, which begins as a muddy black color (②), gradually turns a translucent blue when stirred (③).

WHAT MAKES A SOLUTION SUPERSATURATED?

If a block of solid material (a crystal) is placed in a dilute solution containing the same substance as the solid, the solid will gradually dissolve because more particles escape from the surface of the solid than return to it. But, as the concentration of dissolved material in the solution increases, the rate of return increases. Finally, the rate of dissolving and that of recrystallization are the same, and a condition of equilibrium is reached. This is a SATURATED SOLUTION. But it is also possible to produce a SUPERSATURATED SOLUTION, and in it more particles will leave the solution than leave the solid, and crystals can be made to grow.

Most solids are more soluble in hot solutions than in cold. If a saturated solution is made up, the solution can be cooled down before it begins to solidify. This is a supersaturated solution. If a crystal of the same chemical composition is introduced, the crystal will grow until the solution returns to its saturated state. In this way good crystals can be grown that show clearly which crystal system they belong to.

① Dilute sulfuric acid

Black copper(II) oxide powder

② Glass rod

③ Blue copper(II) sulfate solution

Demonstration 2: growing seed crystals

To grow large, regularly shaped crystals, as shown in demonstrations 3 and 4, "seed" crystals are required.

To prepare seed crystals, part of the solution prepared in demonstration 1 is placed in a Petri dish and the solution evaporated either by leaving it in air or by warming it from below to speed up evaporation. A large number of small copper(II) sulfate crystals will form over the bottom of the Petri dish. This may take hours or days.

Alternatively, a saturated solution of copper(II) sulfate can be prepared by adding copper(II) sulfate crystals to hot water until no more will dissolve. The solution is then allowed to cool, prompting the copper(II) sulfate solution to become supersaturated. Eventually, the entire solution forms into small crystals (④).

A few perfectly formed specimens need to be taken out of this crystallizing solution and used as seed crystals for the growth of large specimens.

Demonstration 3: growing large, regularly shaped copper(II) sulfate crystals in a beaker

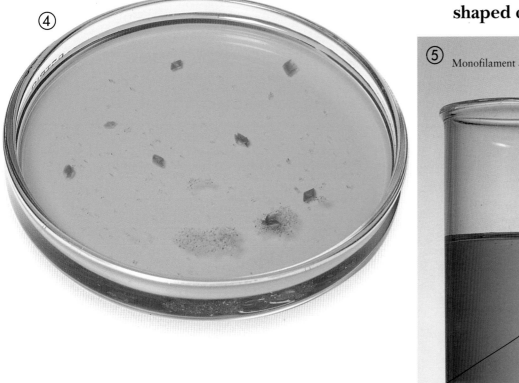

④

⑤ Monofilament

Seed crystal attached to filament

For this technique a small seed crystal is suspended in a supersaturated solution of copper sulfate(II) in a beaker.

The seed crystal is first carefully dried on tissue paper. It is then stuck to a small strand of monofilament fishing thread using a superglue (⑤). The seed crystal acts as a focus for the deposition of more copper ions and sulfate ions from

⑥

the solution, and it grows into a large crystal. It needs to be left suspended in the solution for some weeks (⑥). This technique produces the most perfectly formed crystals (⑦ & ⑧).

A perfect rhombohedral copper(II) sulfate crystal

⑦

This large group of crystals was grown by suspending a seed crystal in a beaker.

⑧

Demonstration 4: growing large, regularly shaped copper(II) sulfate crystals in a Petri dish

To save the trouble of having to suspend a crystal, a seed crystal can be dropped into a saturated solution of copper(II) sulfate in a Petri dish (⑨). The crystal will grow over the following weeks (⑩). However, because the crystal is growing on the glass surface of the Petri dish, it will not form perfect, three-dimensional crystals, but will have one flat side (⑪). Copper(II) sulfate crystals are triclinic (see page 11).

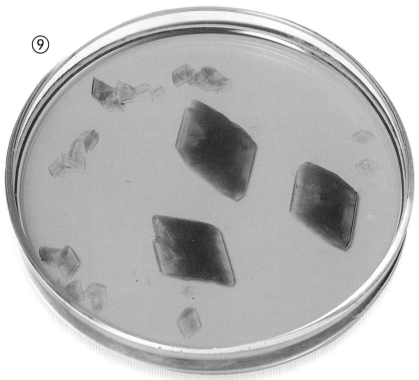

This crystal was grown in a Petri dish. The curved surface shows where it lay on the glass surface.

Water of crystallization

Some solids take up water, forming crystalline structures. This is called WATER OF CRYSTALLIZATION. Hydrated samples of a solid (which contain the maximum amount of water) can be obtained by producing solid crystals by partially evaporating a solution.

Thus, when sodium sulfate (Na_2SO_4) is dissolved in hot water and cooled, crystals of hydrated sodium sulfate decahydrate ($Na_2SO_4 \bullet 10H_2O$) will begin to grow. Similarly, as copper(II) sulfate crystals grow, these are the hydrated form of the compound, ($Cu_2SO_4 \bullet 5H_2O$, copper(II) sulfate pentahydrate) (see pages 14 to 17).

The water in the crystals can be driven off by heating to produce a dry or ANHYDROUS solid.

Demonstration 1: heating hydrated sodium carbonate crystals

Many compounds can be heated to drive off the water of crystallization, changing them from a hydrated form to an anhydrous form. To show that a hydrated solid contains water, some hydrated crystals of translucent sodium carbonate decahydrate are heated ($Na_2CO_3 \bullet 10H_2O$) (①). Within a few seconds the solid begins to melt, then boil, and steam is given off (②). The presence of water from this change can be tested for because it turns blue cobalt(II) chloride pink. The white powder that remains when the steam stops being evolved is anhydrous sodium carbonate (Na_2CO_3).

If the hydrated crystals are exposed to air (③), they turn to a white anhydrous powder – they are said to EFFLORESCE (④).

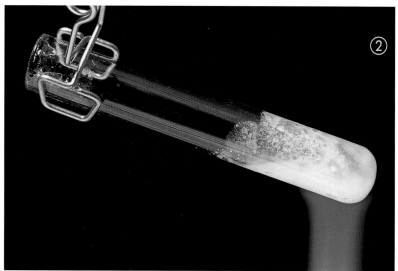

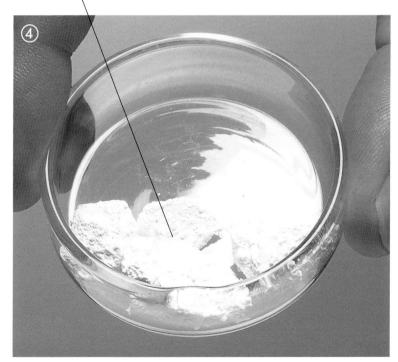

Translucent sodium carbonate decahydrate ($NaCO_3 \cdot 10H_2O$)

Anhydrous sodium carbonate ($NaCO_3$)

Demonstration 2: heating hydrated copper(II) sulfate crystals

If a sample of copper(II) sulfate crystals (obtained as in the demonstration on page 17) is heated, it changes from dark blue to almost white, and at the same time it loses its crystalline structure and decomposes into a powder (⑤).

Remarks

The anhydrous form of compounds that contain water of crystallization readily absorb moisture to reassume their hydrated condition. Some will change color at the same time. Copper(II) sulfate changes from white to blue, and cobalt(II) chloride ($CoCl_2$) from purple to pink, as water is absorbed. Because of this visible change in color, they can be used to test for, or even remove, moisture in a laboratory experiment.

Light blue to white anhydrous copper(II) sulfate powder, ($CuSO_4$)

Dark blue hydrated copper(II) sulfate crystals, ($CuSO_4 \cdot 5H_2O$)

DIFFUSION AND OSMOSIS

In any fluid, whether gas or liquid, particles are moving around, randomly, colliding and bouncing off each other or the walls of their container. When two liquids or two gases are placed in contact, this random movement continues, so that, over time, the particles of each of the two gases (see page 26) or each of the two liquids (see page 33) may become intermixed. This process is called DIFFUSION.

The rate of diffusion is also controlled by the energy that the particles have, so that the more energy they have, the faster they move. Thus diffusion occurs most rapidly in gases and at a much slower rate in liquids, and diffusion is much faster in hot fluids than in cold fluids.

Diffusion rates vary depending on the concentration of molecules. Thus the molecules move from a region where they are in high concentration to areas in which their concentration is lower (see page 22). This difference in concentration is known as the concentration gradient, so that the greater the difference in concentration between two regions, the faster molecules diffuse from the region of the higher to the region of lower concentration.

Also, because light molecules travel faster than heavy ones, the diffusion of light molecules occurs more quickly than the diffusion of heavy molecules (see pages 28 and 30).

The gases and other particles in air are diffusing continually among one another. Thus you may detect a smell at one moment, only to discover that diffusion has quickly dispersed the scent molecules. This is of advantage if the smell is unpleasant!

The rapid rate of diffusion in gases also highlights one reason why fume chambers with strong fans are used. If the fans were not working, diffusion would quickly bring poisonous fumes out into the laboratory.

(Above) The gases emitted from these car exhausts diffuse into the air. Diffusion is sufficiently rapid for the gases to fill the atmosphere over a city very soon after peak traffic flows. The temperature, the atmospheric pressure, concentration of other gases in the atmosphere, and certain other atmospheric conditions all affect the rate of diffusion and how the pollution behaves.

Osmosis in liquids

OSMOSIS is a process that occurs when the SOLVENT (liquid) in a solution passes through a SEMIPERMEABLE MEMBRANE (a form of sieve with microscopically small holes) separating two solutions of different concentration. The osmosis stops as the pressure builds up. It may continue until the two solutions are of equal concentration.

The most commonly witnessed osmosis is when the solvent is water (see page 34). The water passes through the semipermeable membrane, but the contained SOLUTE cannot. As a result, if pure water (pure solvent) and an AQUEOUS solution of sodium chloride (a solution of water as the solvent and sodium chloride as the solute) are connected by a semi-permeable membrane, the level of the solution rises and that of the pure water drops. Some of the pure water has migrated into the sodium chloride solution.

The movement is not a simple diffusion but a more rapid movement caused by unequal pressures on either side of the membrane.

The increase in height of the liquid that occurs on one side of the semipermeable membrane, compared with the other, is a measure of the pressure that osmosis can create. It is known as the osmotic pressure.

Amedeo Avogadro

Amedeo Avogadro (1776–1856) was an Italian count and one of the founders of modern physical chemistry, although during his lifetime his achievement was not recognized.

He began his career as a lawyer, but then he took private lessons in mathematics and science and decided to change career direction. He became a professor of physics in Turin, but he had wide-ranging interests that took him into the field of chemistry.

He is most famous for his law, originally called Avogadro's Hypothesis, which states that equal volumes of all gases, under the same pressure and temperature conditions, contain the same number of molecules. This is an important conclusion that helps to explain many of the physical properties of gases. He also made the suggestion that some molecules might contain only one element (as later shown to be true in the case of oxygen (O_2), etc.).

He knew of experiments (later called ELECTROLYSIS) that showed that when an electric current is passed through water, twice as much hydrogen by volume is produced as oxygen. From this he reasoned that a molecule of water must contain two atoms of hydrogen for every one of oxygen. Then, because the weight of the oxygen gas collected is eight times that of hydrogen gas collected, the oxygen atoms must be 16 times as heavy as those of hydrogen.

Because he was not part of the mainstream scientific community, this important work was not recognized when it was published in 1811 and was only respected when it was reread in 1860, four years after his death. One of the people who heard this second reading was Julius Meyer. He was inspired by these conclusions to put forward his periodic law that was later to be used by Mendeleev to build the PERIODIC TABLE of the elements.

One of the reasons Avogadro's work was ignored is because, at the same time, it had been shown that two similarly charged particles repelled. Therefore people could not believe that molecules existed containing the same particles. We now know that the force holding atoms very close together is stronger than the electrical force repelling them.

Diffusion of gases into a vacuum

Gas molecules travel very rapidly, often at over 500 meters per second. However, the rate at which a gas spreads out (diffuses) in air at normal pressure is slow because many collisions occur with the gas molecules already present in the air. This is why, for example, a smell appears to waft across a room rather than arrive as soon as it is created. Compare the rate of diffusion in this demonstration, where the gas is introduced into a partial vacuum – and so is not slowed down by other gas molecules – with the rate shown in the demonstration on page 26.

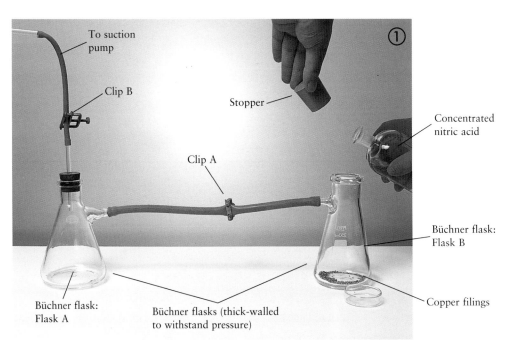

Demonstration: diffusion of nitrogen dioxide into a partial vacuum

The apparatus consists of two BÜCHNER FLASKS (which are made of glass with very thick walls to withstand a near vacuum without breaking), connected together by a length of thin-walled rubber tubing (①). Thin-walled tubing is used so that we can see where the vacuum is forming through the collapse of the tubing.

To separate the two flasks while the vacuum is being created, a clip is closed on the tube between the two Büchner flasks (Clip A).

A further length of thick-walled rubber tubing connects one flask (Flask A) to a standard water-driven laboratory suction pump. The suction pump is started up, and as a partial VACUUM is created, the tubing between clip A and flask B becomes flat.

Now the tube to the suction pump is closed using another clip (Clip B), and the pump is disconnected. Now a partial vacuum has been created in the left-hand part of the apparatus.

To observe the diffusion, a colored gas is needed in the flask farthest from the pump (Flask B). Any colored gas could be used, but for this demonstration nitrogen dioxide was used. However, because nitrogen dioxide is a poisonous gas, the demonstration is conducted in a fume chamber.

To produce the nitrogen dioxide, concentrated nitric acid is poured onto copper in the form of filings, and a stopper is used to seal the flask (②). The gas in Flask B becomes a deep brown within a few seconds, as more and more nitrogen dioxide molecules are added to the air molecules already present. The pressure in the flask will build up above atmospheric pressure. This change in pressure does not affect Flask A because of Clip A that divides Flask A and B along the connecting tubing.

The tubing connecting the flasks is now pinched tightly between the fingers, and the clip removed (③). By quickly unpinching the tubing, the two flasks are suddenly connected (④, see page 25). Nitrogen dioxide appears in flask B almost instantaneously, thus proving that gas molecules can diffuse down the narrow tubing extremely rapidly.

The fact that the direct effect of the pump on increasing diffusion is only slight can be demonstrated by restarting the pump and unclamping the tube connecting the pump to Flask A. The color in Flask A becomes slightly lighter, but the gases are all not immediately evacuated.

Remarks

The pump acts as a one-way valve. At the start of the demonstration gas particles (molecules of the gases in the air — mainly O_2 and N_2) are moving in all directions inside Flask A, and at any instant some are

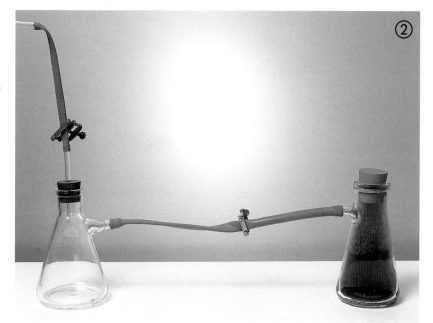

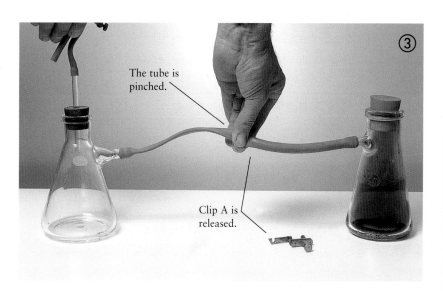

The tube is pinched.

Clip A is released.

down the tube to the pump and pass out of the flask. No particles can reenter while the pump is operating. As a result, the number of gas molecules in Flask A and the connecting tubing decreases as time goes by. By contrast, the number of gas molecules in the air outside the tubing remains the same, and so their greater pressure on the outside of the tubing causes the tubing to collapse.

The chemical reaction in Flask B forms molecules of nitrogen dioxide (NO_2), which are brown. Note that if too much nitrogen dioxide is allowed to form in Flask B, so many molecules of nitrogen dioxide will hit the stopper (the gas pressure inside the flask will increase to such an extent) that the stopper can be hurled out of the flask. This means that the proportion of reagents has to be chosen so that only a sufficient amount of gas is produced.

When Clip A is released, enough molecules move very quickly (at 500 meters per second) into Flask A that it appears to turn brown instantly. This is possible because there are relatively few molecules of gas in Flask A, since most have been evacuated by the suction pump. As a result, the movement of the nitrogen dioxide molecules is not hindered greatly.

EQUATION: Preparation of nitrogen dioxide
Copper + nitric acid ⇨ copper nitrate + water + nitrogen dioxide
$Cu(s) + 4HNO_3(conc) ⇨ Cu(NO_3)_2(aq) + 2H_2O(l) + 2NO_2(g)$

Diffusion of gases at normal pressure

Gases contain more energy than either liquids or solids. Gas molecules are continually moving around, colliding and bouncing off each other to fill the space they are in.

If a gas is introduced to a vacuum, the molecules will occupy the space fastest since there are no other molecules to obstruct their movement (as shown on page 22).

If a gas is introduced into another container at normal pressure conditions, the process of diffusion and mixing is slower, but still much more rapid than in liquids. At normal pressure there are other gas molecules present in the container that are also moving around continually, and these slow the progress of the introduced gas. However, if gases are brought into contact with one another, they will always mix.

Demonstration: diffusion of bromine and air

In this demonstration bromine is used as the introduced gas because it is brown and will not react with air. It is also denser than air. Bromine is poisonous, and so the entire demonstration is performed in a fume chamber.

Bromine is a brown liquid just below room temperature, so that, when some drops are placed in the bottom of a gas jar, molecules of brown bromine vapor (gas) quickly escape from the liquid surface (①).

As soon as a few droplets of bromine liquid have been placed in the gas jar, the top of the jar is sealed with a glass cover slip. Now the bromine is left to evaporate, so that the resulting bromine vapor can come in contact, diffuse, and mix with the air in the gas jar.

The bromine vapor is six times denser than air, and so initially it hugs the bottom of the jar. Because bromine is denser than air, you might

①

Bromine liquid evaporates to produce bromine vapor.

②

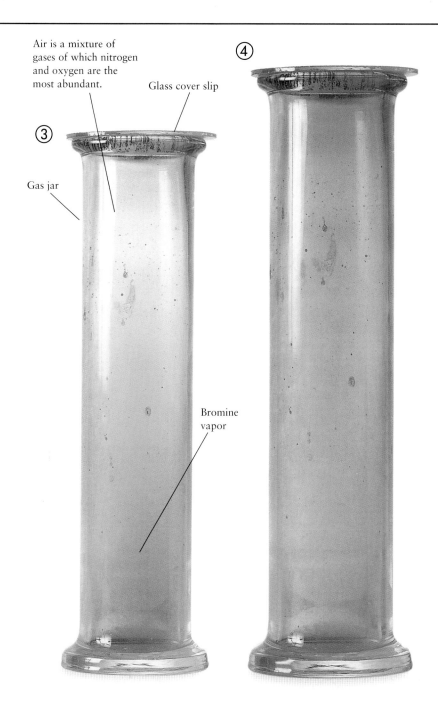

Air is a mixture of gases of which nitrogen and oxygen are the most abundant.

④

③

Glass cover slip

Gas jar

Bromine vapor

expect the gas to remain at the bottom of the jar. The pictures show what actually happened 15 minutes (②), 45 minutes (③), and 5 hours (④) after the liquid was introduced (compare this with the rate of diffusion of liquids on page 32). At the end of this period the bromine molecules have mixed thoroughly with the air molecules, and the jar appears uniformly brown. At the end of this period the bromine and air molecules have collided and intermingled sufficiently to have produced a uniform MIXTURE. The molecules continue to move around at the same rate, but the proportions of each gas anywhere in the jar are now the same, and so the jar stays uniformly brown.

In this demonstration gravity has slowed the diffusion because of the density of the bromine. Nonetheless, the molecules of bromine vapor were sufficiently energetic to operate against the force of gravity and to mix thoroughly.

Remarks

In any mixture of gases the total pressure exerted by each of the gases is equal to the sum of the partial pressures produced by each of the gases. The way bromine diffuses through the air may help you to see why this property might be true.

(Note: Other dense gases, such as yellow-green chlorine, could also be used for this demonstration.)

Diffusion rates and the mass of gas molecules

The demonstrations on pages 22 to 26 of this book have shown that diffusion of gases is rapid when there are few molecules to resist movement, and how diffusion will still occur, but is slowed down, when other molecules are present.

This demonstration shows more accurately that less dense molecules diffuse more quickly than more dense molecules.

In this demonstration two gases whose molecules are of different densities are used to show that gases of light molecules move more quickly than gases of dense molecules.

Demonstration: diffusion of ammonia and hydrogen chloride gas

This demonstration uses the two gases hydrogen chloride and ammonia.

Hydrogen chloride is an acid gas, whereas ammonia is an alkaline gas. It is convenient that when they are in contact, they react to form a white smoke that consists of minute particles of the salt ammonium chloride. Thus the position of the white smoke can be used to show accurately where the gases meet, and therefore what their relative rates of diffusion are.

A long glass tube is mounted horizontally (①). A small amount of hydrogen chloride solution (as concentrated hydrochloric acid) and ammonia (as concentrated ammonia solution) are placed in

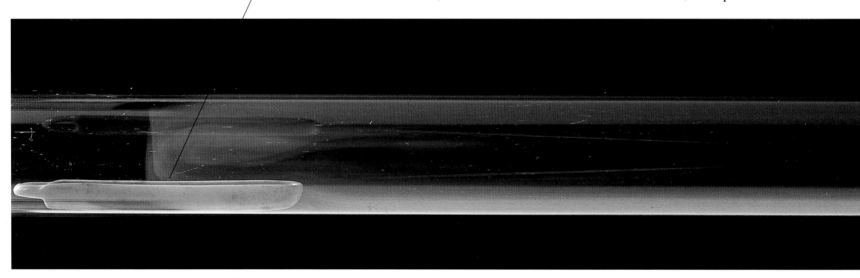

Ceramic boat

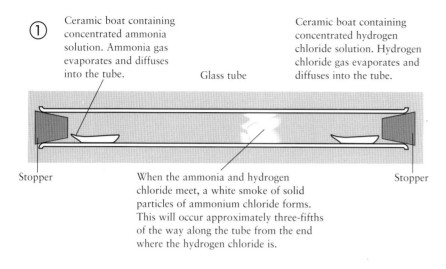

① Ceramic boat containing concentrated ammonia solution. Ammonia gas evaporates and diffuses into the tube.

Glass tube

Ceramic boat containing concentrated hydrogen chloride solution. Hydrogen chloride gas evaporates and diffuses into the tube.

Stopper

When the ammonia and hydrogen chloride meet, a white smoke of solid particles of ammonium chloride forms. This will occur approximately three-fifths of the way along the tube from the end where the hydrogen chloride is.

Stopper

EQUATION: The result of diffusion of hydrogen chloride and ammonia

Hydrogen chloride gas+ ammonia gas ⇨ ammonium chloride (solid)

$HCl(g) + NH_3(g) \Rightarrow NH_4Cl(s)$

Particles of ammonium chloride settle on the wall of the tube.

ceramic "boats," and these are pushed into the ends of the glass tube.

Once the reagents have been introduced, the ends of the tube are sealed with stoppers. Each of the reagents now begins to vaporize, and diffusion proceeds from the two ends of the tube. Both the hydrogen chloride and the ammonia have to diffuse through the air in the tube before they can diffuse into each other, react, and produce a dense white smoke as a precipitate (②).

In this demonstration, which was performed in a 1-meter-long tube, it took 7 minutes before white smoke was produced. The smoke formed about 60 cm from the ammonia boat. This suggests that ammonia molecules, which are only half as dense as hydrogen chloride molecules, diffused 1.5 times as quickly as hydrogen chloride.

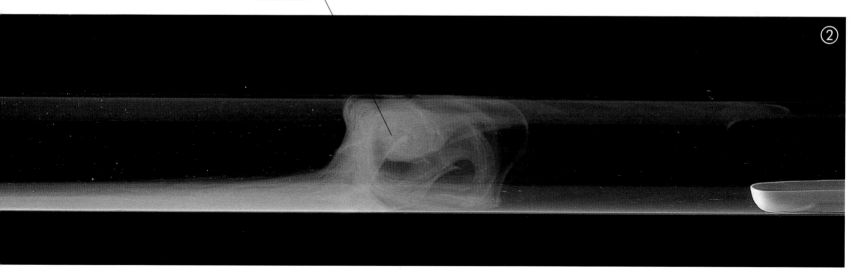

②

Diffusion and the density of gas molecules

All the gas molecules of a particular gas have a fixed size. Whether a gas will diffuse through a porous membrane or not depends on the size of the holes (pores) in the membrane and the size of the gas molecules.

In this demonstration a porous pot is used. This is a ceramic container that has very small pores of uniform size. For this demonstration a porous pot has been chosen that has pores that are just larger than the size of oxygen (relative atomic mass 32) and nitrogen molecules (relative atomic mass 28), the main gases in the air. The rates at which these gases diffuse will be compared with hydrogen (relative atomic mass 2), the least dense of all gases.

Demonstration: diffusion of hydrogen

A hollow, porous pot, consisting of a closed cylinder of porous ceramic, has a tube leading from the chamber. This tube is connected to a U-shaped glass tube, and the U-tube is then partly filled with dilute potassium permanganate solution in such a way as to form a MANOMETER. (The potassium permanganate is used only because it is easy to see.) (①)

A manometer is a U-tube partly filled with liquid and designed to measure changes in gas pressure. The difference in pressures is shown by the level of liquid in each arm of the tube; the tube where the liquid level is lowest is subject to the greater gas pressure. The liquid levels come to rest when the excess gas pressure is balanced by the pressure due to the difference in height between the columns of liquid.

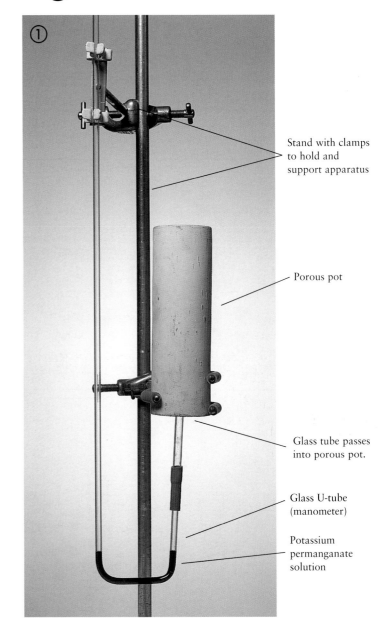

①

Stand with clamps to hold and support apparatus

Porous pot

Glass tube passes into porous pot.

Glass U-tube (manometer)

Potassium permanganate solution

At the start of the demonstration the liquid levels in the two arms of the manometer are the same, indicating that the air pressure inside the porous pot is the same as the surrounding atmospheric air pressure; that is, air molecules are entering and leaving the porous pot at the same rate.

A glass jar just a little larger than the porous pot is now filled with hydrogen gas. The hydrogen is prepared by reacting dilute hydrochloric acid with zinc. Hydrogen is lighter than air, and so the glass jar is kept inverted throughout the demonstration (②).

When the glass jar containing hydrogen is placed over the porous pot, the colored liquid in the manometer immediately rises up the tube (③). This is because hydrogen molecules start to diffuse through the pores of the pot (the concentration of hydrogen molecules inside the pot is far less than the concentration of hydrogen molecules in the jar). At the same time, molecules of oxygen and nitrogen attempt to diffuse out of the pot into the glass jar because the concentration of oxygen and nitrogen in the jar (which is filled with hydrogen) is low.

Because hydrogen molecules have low mass, they can pass through the pores of the porous pot much more quickly than the molecules of nitrogen or oxygen. As a result, the porous pot becomes crowded with molecules, the pressure builds up at the exit tube, and the liquid is pushed up the manometer.

Beaker containing hydrogen gas

②

Glass cover slip

③

Potassium permanganate solution rises up the U-tube.

The glass jar containing the hydrogen is placed over the porous pot.

Exit tube

When the jar is slightly lifted off the porous pot, the liquid not only returns to the bottom of the manometer but then rises up the tube toward the porous pot ((4)).

The hydrogen inside the porous pot quickly diffuses through the pot and escapes to the atmosphere. Nitrogen and oxygen molecules from the air cannot diffuse into the pot as quickly as the hydrogen is diffusing out. Thus there is now a shortage of molecules in the porous pot, and the difference in pressure on the arms of the liquid in the U-tube pushes the liquid up the manometer limb connected to the porous pot.

Diffusion in liquids

As with gases, when two different liquids are placed in contact, they start to mix, one diffusing into the other. However, the rate at which they do this is perhaps four orders of magnitude (ten thousand times) slower than in gases. Any demonstration that involves diffusion of liquids therefore has to be planned to last over several months, the apparatus being set up, the liquids brought carefully into contact, and then the liquids set aside in an unused (an evenly heated) part of the laboratory where the diffusion can proceed undisturbed.

Demonstration: diffusion of potassium permanganate solution

In this demonstration the solutions used are concentrated potassium permanganate solution and water. Potassium permanganate is used because it is soluble in water and retains its color at very low concentrations. It is also cheap and readily available. Concentrated copper sulfate solution is a good alternative.

The potassium permanganate solution is made up and put to one side. The water to be used is put into the gas jar and also put to one side. After several hours the temperatures of the two solutions will be the same.

Pipette is used to introduce the concentrated potassium permanganate solution.

Water has been left to stand and cool.

The key to this demonstration is to introduce one liquid into the other without disturbance. This is achieved with great care, using a pipette to introduce the more dense potassium permanganate into the bottom of a gas jar that had previously been filled with water (①).

The diffusion can then be observed over the following weeks (②) and months (③).

Remarks

Although this demonstration is very simple, good results are very difficult to achieve in an ordinary laboratory. This is because there are so many factors that can disturb such slow diffusion. One of the most common is that changes in temperature within the laboratory may well set up convection currents within the solution. Convection currents can easily be more dominant than diffusion in this situation.

Osmosis

Osmosis is an important property of solutions that are in contact through a semipermeable membrane, but which have different concentrations of solute (see also page 21).

Demonstration: osmosis into glucose solution

This demonstration uses a piece of special viscose tubing (made from cellulose) that is commonly available in biology laboratories as a semipermeable membrane. (Osmosis is a particularly important process in nature and is often demonstrated by biologists.)

First, a glucose solution is prepared by dissolving glucose (a solute) in distilled water. A yellow dye is added to this solution so that we can see what is happening.

The viscose tubing is fixed onto the end of a glass tube and clamped at the other so as to seal the tubing and make a bag. The glucose solution and dye mixture are then passed down the tubing until they fill the viscose membrane and are some way up the tube.

The tube and viscose tubing are lowered into a beaker containing distilled water and held vertically with a clamp (①).

During the next few minutes the level of the liquid in the tubing begins to rise, then stabilizes (②).

Remarks

The nature of osmosis is demonstrated here with water as the solvent. The viscose tubing has pores of such a size that water molecules can move through it, but the larger glucose and dye molecules cannot. Initially, the water molecules are

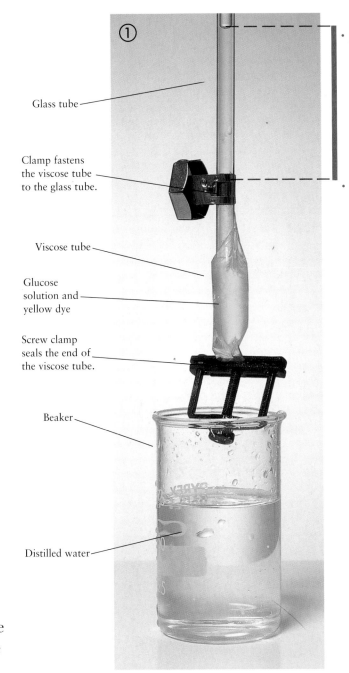

① Glass tube

Clamp fastens the viscose tube to the glass tube.

Viscose tube

Glucose solution and yellow dye

Screw clamp seals the end of the viscose tube.

Beaker

Distilled water

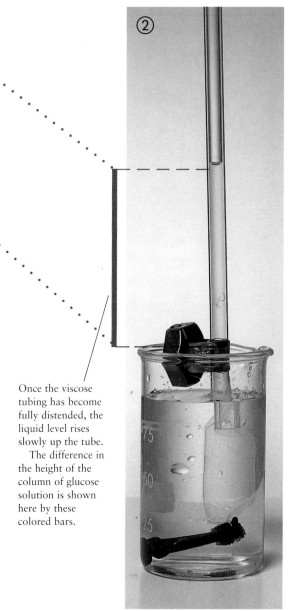

in very much higher concentration in the water than in the glucose solution, and so there is a concentration gradient across the viscose tubing (③).

Over time the water molecules move through the membrane from the beaker, where they are in high concentration, to the glucose solution, where they are in low concentration, to address this imbalance (④).

As the water molecules flow into the glucose solution, the viscose tubing begins to expand. Once it has expanded to its full capacity, the excess liquid produced by the continued migration of water causes the level of the solution to rise in the glass tubing. Eventually, the pressure produced by this osmosis effect is balanced by the pressure due to the height of water in the tubing, and then the level of liquid in the tubing stabilizes.

Once the viscose tubing has become fully distended, the liquid level rises slowly up the tube.

The difference in the height of the column of glucose solution is shown here by these colored bars.

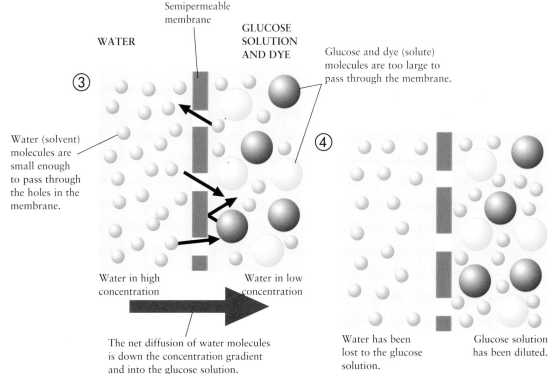

Semipermeable membrane

WATER

GLUCOSE SOLUTION AND DYE

Glucose and dye (solute) molecules are too large to pass through the membrane.

③

Water (solvent) molecules are small enough to pass through the holes in the membrane.

④

Water in high concentration

Water in low concentration

The net diffusion of water molecules is down the concentration gradient and into the glucose solution.

Water has been lost to the glucose solution.

Glucose solution has been diluted.

35

PHASE CHANGES

Substances can exist as gases, liquids, and solids. Each of these states of a substance is also called a PHASE; so we can speak of a solid phase, a liquid phase, or a gaseous phase. When a substance changes to another phase, this is called a PHASE CHANGE.

Phase changes are common occurrences and are shown in the diagram on page 6. For example, a change from liquid to gas phase is called evaporation, or vaporization (boiling is a special case, see page 6 and page 56); the reverse is called condensation. A change from liquid to solid phase is called solidification (and in the case of water, freezing), while a change from solid phase to liquid phase is called melting (①) (see pages 38 and 42). Some substances can also change from a solid directly to a gas or vice versa. This kind of phase change is called sublimation (see page 50).

Substances change from one phase to another as energy is gained or lost. The phase with the lowest energy state is a solid, which is why substances solidify as they cool. The phase with the highest energy state is a gas.

In chemistry we are often interested in the temperature at which these changes in phase occur, such as the melting point (pages 52, 54, and 64), the freezing point (page 52), and the boiling point (page 56). The temperature of these changes can be affected by the presence of impurities (page 62 and 63).

(Above) The white solid phase of lead bromide ($PbBr_2$) can be melted to form its liquid phase when heated with a Bunsen burner flame.

Distinguishing between melting a substance and dissolving it

Melting a substance is a phase change and is the result of adding energy such as heat.

However, when a substance dissolves in a liquid, there is no phase change. The particles of the solid just break up and intermingle with the liquid. In chemistry the solid is a solute that has dissolved in a solvent to make a solution. The solution contains the solute and solvent. The solid has not melted but, instead, has dissolved in the solvent, which is already in its liquid phase.

Crystalline potassium dichromate (②) is very stable in heat and will only melt if heated to a very high temperature. However, the same crystal (a solute) will dissolve in water (a solvent) on a laboratory bench (③).

So you make a phase change by changing the temperature (and sometimes the pressure) of a substance without the presence of any other substance, whereas you dissolve a substance in a solvent, and there is no phase change.

② Solid potassium dichromate

Many solutions are used in the laboratory.

If water is dripped across a solid potassium dichromate crystal, some of the solid (solute) dissolves in the water (a solvent) to produce an aqueous solution (potassium dichromate in water) This is represented in chemical equations by the symbol (aq).

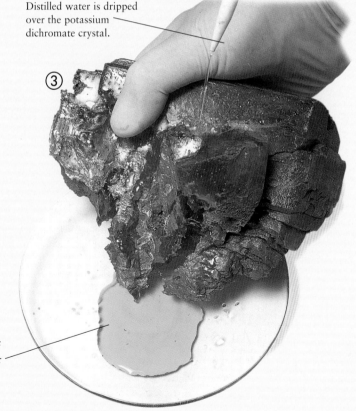

Distilled water is dripped over the potassium dichromate crystal.

③

Phase changes in sulfur

By heating and then cooling sulfur, some phase changes can be investigated and explained in terms of the structure of its molecules.

Demonstration: investigating the phase changes of sulfur

Native, or pure, solid sulfur contains only atoms of the element sulfur. In a solid powder phase these atoms are bonded together as molecules of eight atoms that are the shape of buckled rings (①).

In this demonstration reagent-quality sulfur powder is placed in a test tube ready for heating (②).

The yellow sulfur powder melts at 115°C. Despite this low melting temperature, it takes a long while for all of the sulfur to melt because sulfur is a poor conductor of heat (③).

Molten sulfur is an amber liquid that is quite runny (it has a low VISCOSITY) (④). The reason for this is that the energy of heating allows the buckled rings to spread apart and flatten enough to slide over each other (⑤).

To imagine how this works, think of a can of spaghetti rings. When cold, the contents of the emptied can will stand up in a saucepan (they act as a solid), but when heated, the rings start to slide around.

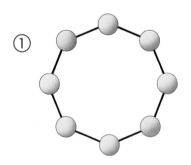

①

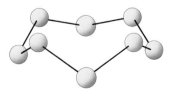

Found in solid sulfur, the buckled ring molecule of sulfur is made of eight atoms of sulfur. From above, they form an octagon, and from the side the regular buckling can be seen.

②

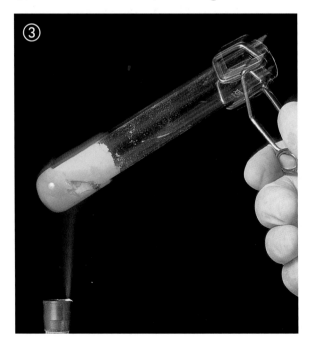

③

When more heat is applied, the sulfur darkens, and the liquid becomes more viscous. When it reaches 187°C, the tube can be turned over, and the liquid will not move (⑥, see page 40). The extra heating has ruptured the rings, and they have formed into chains that are now entangled. (Compare the entangling to strands of spaghetti that have been stirred vigorously.)

Heat even further (to 444°C), and the sulfur turns black (⑦, see page 40). The sulfur becomes liquid again because it has reached its boiling point. The extra heat energy has ruptured the chains, and they now lie in short lengths that can easily move about. (Compare this to chopping each spaghetti ring once around its edge.)

The liquid can now be poured into cold water, where it solidifies. When picked out of the water, it can be pulled about like plastic (⑧ & ⑨, see page 41).

The crash-cooling has taken away energy quickly, causing the sulfur to form enormously long chains (it has POLYMERIZED) (⑩). As the plastic sulfur is molded between the fingers, some energy is added, and the structure returns to rings, gradually turning back to a brittle, yellow solid.

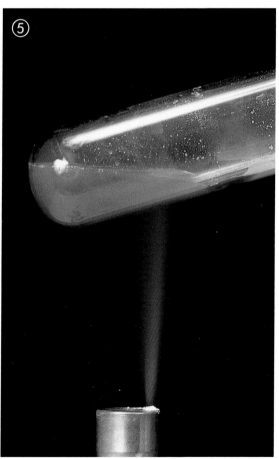

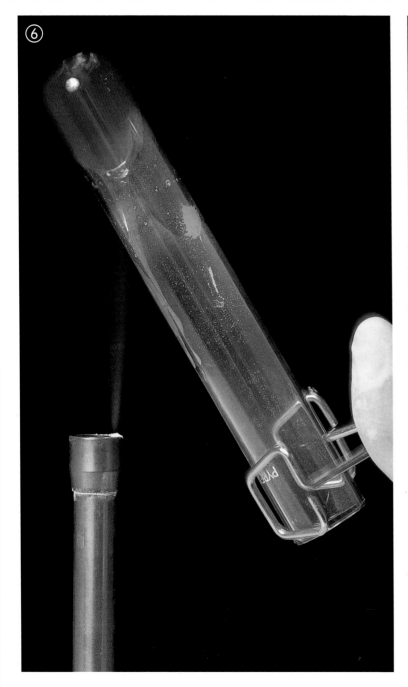

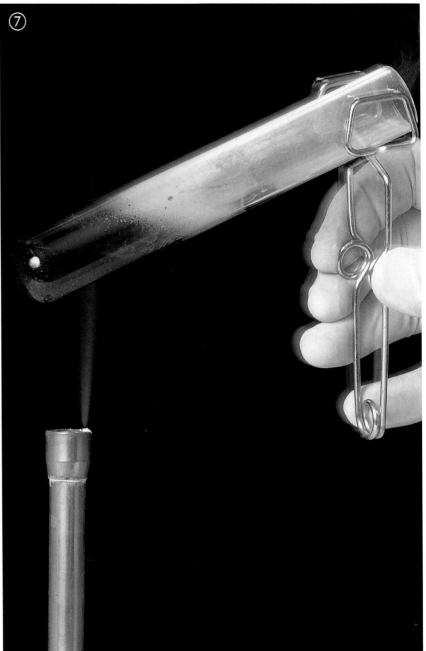

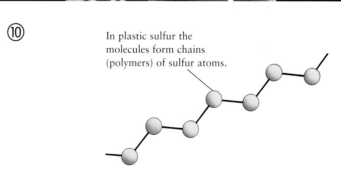

In plastic sulfur the molecules form chains (polymers) of sulfur atoms.

41

Phase changes with gentle heating

The way in which substances change between their solid, liquid, and gas phases depends, in part, on the rate at which they are heated and the way in which they cool. Many substances behave in quite unexpected ways, as these next demonstrations with gentle heating and slow cooling show. Observing the changes carefully is the key to understanding the processes at work.

The next three demonstrations use several substances with low melting points, which can therefore be melted using steam from boiling water. This is one of the slowest and most gentle forms of heating, only reaching about 100°C. In each case the substance is placed on a watch glass. The watch glass rests on a beaker about two-thirds full of boiling water, which stands on a tripod and is heated with a Bunsen flame.

Demonstration 1: melting of acetamide

The first substance under observation is acetamide as white crystals. As the crystals are heated, they melt to form a colorless liquid (①) (this is the liquid phase of the substance and not a solution).

Melting means that the particles have received enough energy from the hot surface of the watch glass to enable them to vibrate and rotate sufficiently to leave the fixed positions they

NOTE: When the water in the beaker is heated strongly, it changes phase from its liquid phase to a gaseous phase (as vapor or steam). Some of the steam condenses on the side of the beaker to form its liquid phase again.

①

Acetamide crystals added using a spatula

Watch glass

Gauze pad

Beaker containing water that is being boiled to produce steam.

Standard laboratory tripod to support apparatus above Bunsen flame

Bunsen Burner to heat the beaker

② Liquid acetamide

had when solid, but the particles still stay quite close together and so form a liquid, not a gas.

Some substances, like acetamide, will not easily recrystallize as they cool. To show this property, the heat is removed from under the beaker. Although the liquid cools, no crystals form (②). However, if the liquid is disturbed in any way, such as by touching it with a metal blade, then it crystallizes quickly (③, see page 44), with needle-shaped crystals growing outward from the place of disturbance (④,⑤, & ⑥, see page 44).

Remarks

Because the solid is made of needles, any one crystal has a relatively small area in contact with the glass, and so it does not adhere to it. The solid can therefore be pushed across the glass quite easily.

Notice also that not only does the acetamide recrystallize, but it crystallizes into the very regular crystal arrangement characteristic of the crystal system to which it belongs rather than into the small broken crystals in which it comes as a reagent.

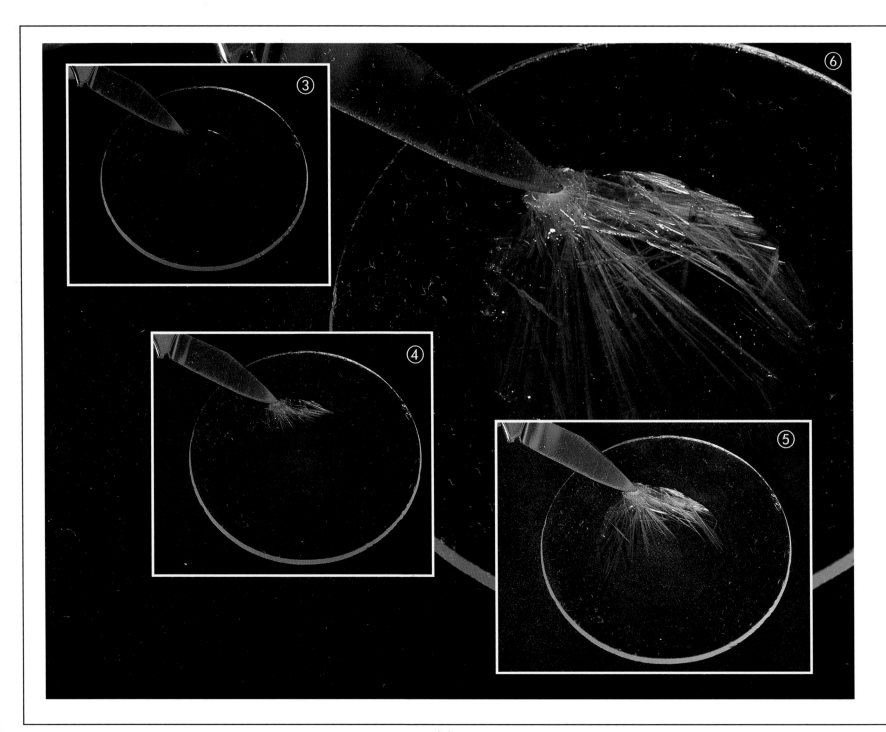

Demonstration 2: melting of naphthalene

As in demonstration 1 for acetamide, naphthalene crystals can also be melted over water using steam. When the molten naphthalene cools, it crystallizes into platelike crystals (⑦), as opposed to the needlelike crystals of ethanamide.

Looking carefully at the pattern of crystals reveals that the lines on the surface of the cooling sample are therefore cracks in the thin crust of solid that has formed over the cooling liquid.

Remarks

Because the recrystallizing solid is made of very thin, flat, platelike crystals, they have a very large surface area in contact with the glass and therefore adhere to it. Thus naphthalene sticks firmly to the glass and can only be removed by remelting it or by dissolving it in a solvent.

Demonstration 3: sublimation and melting of camphor

This demonstration, which uses TRANSLUCENT white crystals of camphor, reveals that although camphor crystals do not melt at the temperature of steam, the particles nevertheless become cemented together. This has occurred because of sublimation. (For the effects of strong heating on camphor, see page 48.)

Camphor has a melting point above 100°C, and so the particles of camphor placed on the watch glass do not melt. However, although the camphor was placed on the watch glass as individual granules (⑧), after a few moments heating, if any of the particles are touched, all the particles move together as though they are all making some kind of raft (⑨). This means that the granular solid has stuck together even though it has not melted. The solid has undergone a localized phase change, sublimation.

The camphor granules have received enough heat energy to allow some of the solid to turn directly to gas. Notice that sublimation has only occurred on the hottest part of the solid, where it touches the watch glass. As soon as the vapor created by sublimation moves away from this high energy region, however, it cools and turns back to solid again. The surfaces of the granules form an easy surface on which to sublime, and in so doing, the sublimating camphor cements the granules where they touch.

Camphor

⑧

Raft of crystals can be pushed around the watch glass.

Phase changes with vigorous heating

How a substance behaves may depend on the rate of heating. Camphor is an example of a substance that can either melt or sublime depending on the rate at which heat energy is applied.

Demonstration: vigorous heating of camphor

As we have seen on page 46, if camphor is heated gently, it begins to sublime, causing granules of solid to cement together.

By contrast, if camphor is strongly heated in a boiling tube, it melts and then almost immediately boils, forming a vapor (①).

There are both physical and chemical changes. The strong heating causes the solid to melt and then vaporize, two physical changes. The vapor is much more chemically reactive than the solid or the liquid, so that it will combust in air if ignited to produce a yellow flame (②). The COMBUSTION results in a chemical change.

Remarks

The reason why all of these different changes of phase can be seen going on at the same time, in the same tube, is connected with the way in which camphor behaves under different degrees of heating.

At the bottom of the boiling tube, where the heating is most vigorous, the camphor boils off as vapor, and the glass is clear. Further up the tube, which receives no direct heat, the camphor vapor cools and sublimes to its solid phase, producing the OPAQUE small crystals that make a white deposit (③).

When the heating is stopped, the liquid at the bottom of the tube cools, crystallizing into an AMORPHOUS, white solid.

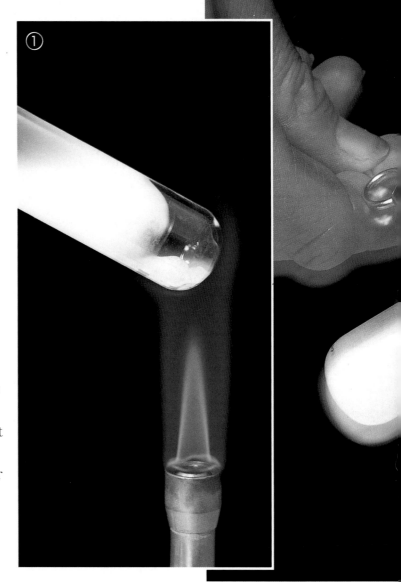

①

Sublimation

Some substances do not have a liquid phase under certain conditions. When they are heated, they change directly from a solid to a vapor or vapor to solid. This change of phase is called sublimation.

Demonstration: sublimation of iodine

In this demonstration solid iodine pellets (crystals) are scattered on the bottom of a flat-bottomed flask (①). A watch glass, rather than a stopper, is placed on top of the flask to prevent loss of too much vapor during heating, but at the same time, to allow the gas to expand. Because iodine vapor is poisonous, the demonstration is performed in a fume chamber.

Shortly after being heated, the iodine crystals in the bottom of the flask sublime, forming a purple vapor (②). The density of the purple vapor increases (③), and at the same time, purple crystals begin to grow on the upper (cooler) parts of the flask (away from the heated base). These are also crystals of iodine since the vapor turns back to the solid phase (④).

Iodine pellets

①

②

Remarks

The growth of crystals depends on the heating conditions in the flask. If the aim is to try to produce large crystals, it is advantageous to have a relatively small amount of iodine vapor in the flask. Thus, by heating the flask moderately, as opposed to vigorously, a steady supply of iodine is made available to the few crystals that begin to form on the upper region of the flask.

If the aim is to produce many small crystals, the iodine is heated more strongly. In this case a very large amount of iodine is available to sublime. Because there is now competition between the crystals for the iodine vapor, a large number are formed that grow to a modest size.

③

④

Iodine crystals

51

Finding the melting point of a solid or freezing point of a liquid

Pure substances have fixed physical properties (constants). This means that, for example, a pure substance will always melt or freeze at the same temperature. As a result, the melting point can also be used to identify a pure substance. (For the effect of impurities on melting point see page 63.)

Demonstration 1: melting point of a solid – sodium thiosulfate

The melting point is the temperature at which a solid turns into a liquid (or a liquid solidifies). Because it is difficult to get a thermometer into a solid substance, it is far more convenient to melt the substance, put a thermometer into the liquid, cool it again, and measure the temperature as the liquid solidifies (①). In this demonstration sodium thiosulfate is melted in a test tube, and a stirring thermometer inserted. The stirring thermometer is used to agitate the liquid and keep a uniform temperature during cooling. The temperature of the sodium thiosulfate is then read from the thermometer.

There are two ways to make sure you have recorded the melting point temperature. First, it is easy to spot the first crystals that form in the liquid as it begins to solidify (②). The temperature is therefore read at this point. Second, the temperature stops dropping for a while during solidification as the liquid turns into the solid phase and releases energy in the form of LATENT HEAT. Thus, if a record is kept of the temperature every 30 seconds, a graph can be plotted of temperature against time (③). The break in the curve

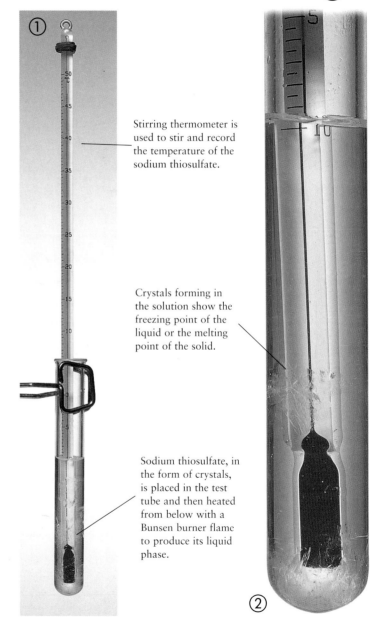

Stirring thermometer is used to stir and record the temperature of the sodium thiosulfate.

Crystals forming in the solution show the freezing point of the liquid or the melting point of the solid.

Sodium thiosulfate, in the form of crystals, is placed in the test tube and then heated from below with a Bunsen burner flame to produce its liquid phase.

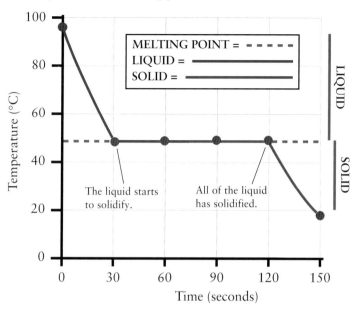

③ *(Below)* The cooling curve of a normal liquid. The horizontal line gives the temperature at the melting point.

MELTING POINT = - - - -
LIQUID = ——————
SOLID = ——————

The liquid starts to solidify.

All of the liquid has solidified.

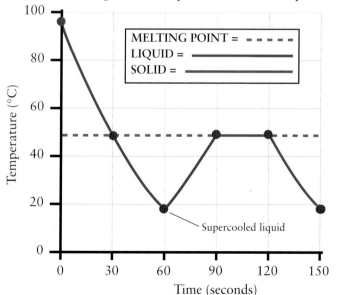

④ *(Below)* The cooling curve of a liquid that will exhibit supercooling.

MELTING POINT = - - - - -
LIQUID = ——————
SOLID = ——————

Supercooled liquid

(noted by a horizontal section) corresponds to the melting point and the period over which latent heat was released. Sodium thiosulfate has a melting point of 48°C.

Demonstration 2: supercooling sodium thiosulfate

Some substances, such as sodium thiosulfate, display the property of SUPERCOOLING. To illustrate this, the liquid must remain undisturbed. A test tube of sodium thiosulfate crystals is once again melted to produce an aqueous solution. Because the water comes only from the crystals, the water released on melting is just enough for the crystals to re-form on cooling.

A stirring thermometer is placed in the liquid. In this case the apparatus is left undisturbed, that is, the thermometer is not agitated in the cooling liquid. The temperature is recorded every half a minute as in demonstration 1.

Because sodium thiosulfate exhibits the property of supercooling, it will cool down to about 20°C without solidifying, provided it is undisturbed, even though its true melting point is 48°C.

If, at this low temperature, a single crystal of sodium thiosulfate is dropped into the solution and the solution stirred, the sodium thiosulfate will begin to crystallize immediately. At the same time, the temperature will rise sharply to 48°C, which is the true melting point temperature. The temperature will then remain constant until all of the latent heat has been released, whereupon the temperature of the solid will begin to fall once more.

Finding the melting point of small samples

The melting point can be used to identify a pure substance. However, in many cases the amount of sample available for test is too small for the method shown on page 52 to be used. Here is an alternative method for finding the melting point of such small samples.

Demonstration: melting point of a small sample

This demonstration uses a short length of CAPILLARY tubing that has been sealed at one end in a Bunsen flame. Using a spatula, a small amount of the sample under test is pushed into the capillary tube. The tube is then tapped to shake the sample down to the closed end of the tube (①).

The demonstration relies on the use of an oil bath, the temperature of which can be raised gradually using a Bunsen flame. Oil, rather than water, is used because water would only be able to melt those substances with very low melting points. Many more substances will melt at temperatures below the boiling point of oil.

In this case, instead of the stirring thermometer being placed inside the tube containing the sample, the tube containing the sample is strapped to the thermometer using an elastic band (②).

The thermometer is clamped and a stirring rod used to ensure that there is an even temperature in the oil bath (③).

The capillary tube is so small that the heat easily penetrates the sample, and it can be assumed that the substance inside the capillary and the thermometer are all at the same temperature.

Now the sample is raised above its melting point. It is usually easy to see even a small sample melt, because the opaque solid suddenly becomes a transparent liquid that runs to the bottom of the tube (④).

The melting point can now be read from the thermometer.

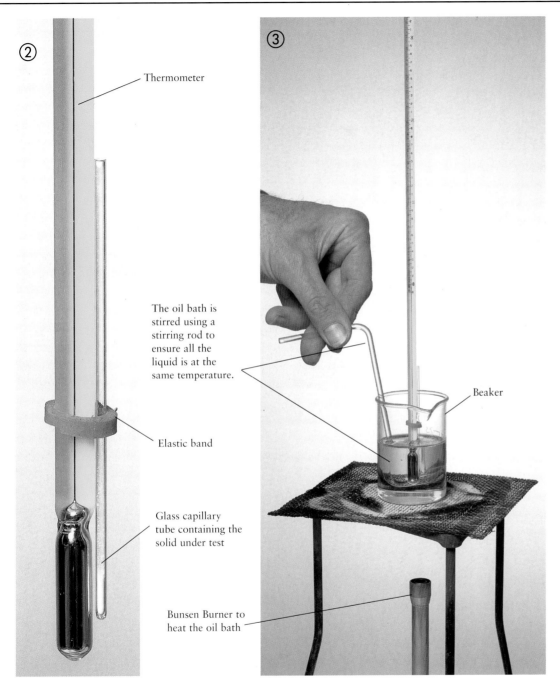

② Thermometer

The oil bath is stirred using a stirring rod to ensure all the liquid is at the same temperature.

③

Elastic band

Glass capillary tube containing the solid under test

Beaker

Bunsen Burner to heat the oil bath

Remarks

It is also often possible to tell whether the sample is pure or impure. If it is pure, all of the substance will melt at the same moment. If melting is slower and occurs over a range of temperatures, then the sample is impure, and the melting point temperature range will have no other meaning.

④

Boiling point of a liquid

The boiling point, just like the melting point, can be used to identify pure substances. However, it is important to realize that boiling point temperatures, unlike melting point temperatures, can be affected by air pressure (see page 58). This demonstration is therefore conducted at ordinary air pressures.

Demonstration: boiling point of distilled water

When a substance boils, the temperature of the boiling liquid is the same as the temperature of the vapor immediately above the boiling surface. However, it is possible to raise the temperature of the boiling liquid above the true boiling point by vigorous heating, and so it is usual to measure the temperature of the vapor rather than the liquid.

This apparatus uses a side-arm, round-bottomed flask. However, any side-arm vessel, such as a side-arm boiling tube, could be used. The important point is that there is a side arm that allows vapor to escape and prevents any buildup of pressure in the flask as the liquid is heated.

Inert sintered-silica antibumping granules are added to the distilled water before it is heated (①). The granules bounce around on the bottom of the flask, and this promotes the formation of small bubbles rather than irregular large ones and therefore reduces the chances of uneven heating.

A thermometer is fitted into the stopper in the neck of the flask, adjusting the position of the bulb of the thermometer so that it is well above the water and thus out of reach of any splashes of boiling water.

The flask is now heated until steady boiling occurs (②). The vapor (steam) produced moves down the side arm and condenses in the cooler air. A small collecting vessel is placed under the end of the side arm to collect the condensation.

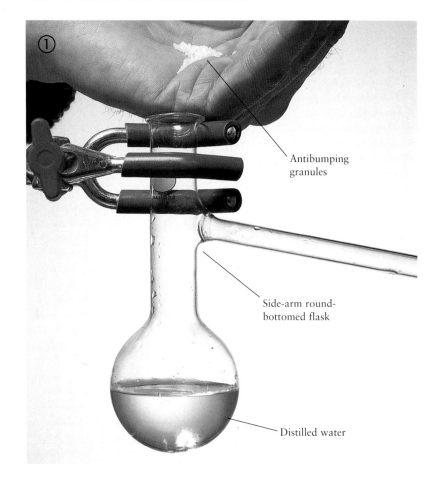

Antibumping granules

Side-arm round-bottomed flask

Distilled water

Thermometer is inserted through a rubber stopper and read every few seconds during heating.

②

③

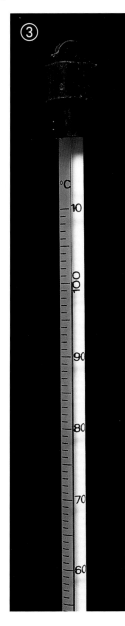

The thermometer is read when it reaches a steady temperature. The steady temperature indicates the boiling point (③).

Remarks

The steady temperature reached at standard atmospheric pressure should be 100°C. If the steady temperature is not 100°C, this is likely to be the effect of atmospheric pressure. Boiling temperatures lower than 100°C will be read if the pressure varies significantly from standard atmospheric pressure of 100 kilopascals (approximately 1 atmosphere), for example, because the demonstration is being conducted at high altitude, or because a low-pressure system is passing nearby. Alternatively, an intense anticyclone will cause an increase in pressure, and readings above 100°C may then be obtained.

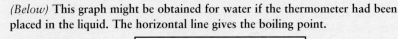

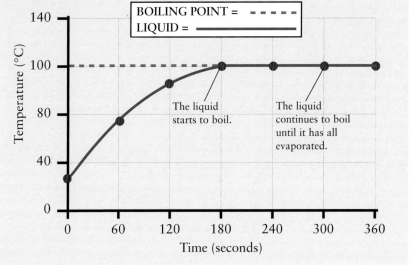

(Below) This graph might be obtained for water if the thermometer had been placed in the liquid. The horizontal line gives the boiling point.

BOILING POINT = - - - - -
LIQUID = ———

The liquid starts to boil.

The liquid continues to boil until it has all evaporated.

Phase changes and pressure

When a substance changes from a liquid to a gas, molecules of vapor are formed that try to occupy a larger space than the liquid. They thus exert an increased pressure. This is illustrated by a classic demonstration using a J-shaped tube.

Demonstration: vapor pressure at boiling point

A J-tube is a piece of narrow glass tubing bent into the shape of a J. It acts as a miniature manometer to measure pressure. It is sealed at one end and open at the other (①).

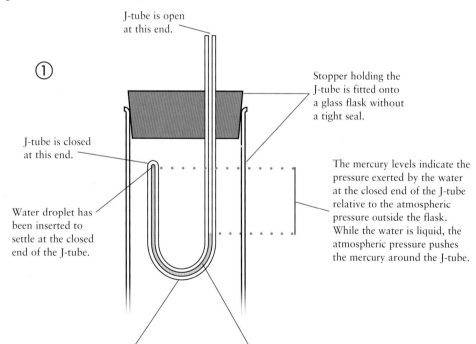

① J-tube is open at this end.

J-tube is closed at this end.

Water droplet has been inserted to settle at the closed end of the J-tube.

J-tube

Mercury

Stopper holding the J-tube is fitted onto a glass flask without a tight seal.

The mercury levels indicate the pressure exerted by the water at the closed end of the J-tube relative to the atmospheric pressure outside the flask. While the water is liquid, the atmospheric pressure pushes the mercury around the J-tube.

The J-tube is first prepared with water and mercury. Mercury is added until the J-tube is about half full. The J-tube is then tilted back and forth until any trapped air bubbles are removed. A small amount of water now has to be inserted in the closed end of the J-tube. This is done using a very small bore, flexible capillary tube that takes the water around the bend of the tube. Because water is less dense than mercury, it will rise automatically to the closed end of the tube. The capillary tube is withdrawn, and the water is thus trapped in the J-tube by the mercury.

The J-tube is pushed into a stopper, which is then fitted to a conical flask containing some distilled water.

At the start of the demonstration air pressure pushes down onto the mercury and the water in the J-tube so that the mercury in the tube is higher on the side containing the water droplet (② and detail).

The flask is now heated so that the water in it boils (③ and detail on page 60). Steam can escape through the gaps around the cork, so the water boils at atmospheric pressure. The boiling water, in turn, causes the water in the end of the J-tube to boil, and as this trapped water turns to vapor, the levels of mercury in

J-tube in a
cork, loose-
fitting stopper

Conical flask

Distilled water
with antibumping
ceramic chips

②

59

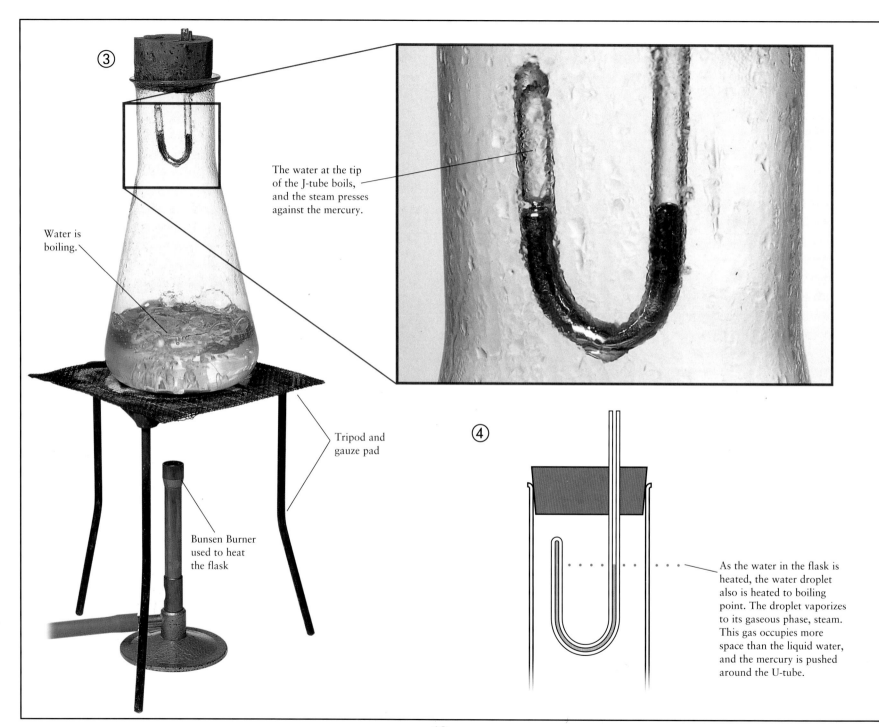

③

The water at the tip of the J-tube boils, and the steam presses against the mercury.

Water is boiling.

Tripod and gauze pad

Bunsen Burner used to heat the flask

④

As the water in the flask is heated, the water droplet also is heated to boiling point. The droplet vaporizes to its gaseous phase, steam. This gas occupies more space than the liquid water, and the mercury is pushed around the U-tube.

both sides of the J-tube become the same, that is, the vapor from the boiling water inside the J-tube is exerting a pressure on the mercury that exactly matches the outside air pressure ((4)).

When the stopper is taken out of the flask ((5), and detail), cool air surrounds the J-tube, and the water vapor condenses. The liquid water occupies a much smaller space than the vapor and so the mercury swings around the J-tube to return to its starting position.

Remarks

Because the volume of the J-tube 1 is small, it responds very quickly to differences in outside temperature. This can be shown by replacing the stopper in the flask for a few seconds. The water in the J-tube will vaporize within a few seconds. If the stopper is removed, the liquid will condense almost immediately.

The demonstration can also be used to show that adding an impurity to the water in the tube reduces the vapor pressure and raises the boiling point. As a result, no movement would be experienced in the J-tube even when the water in the flask was boiling strongly. This can happen if the mercury used is not pure and contains some water-soluble impurities.

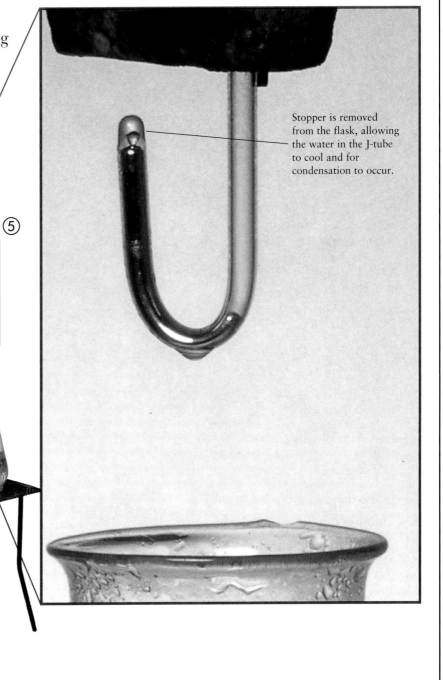

(5)

Stopper is removed from the flask, allowing the water in the J-tube to cool and for condensation to occur.

The effect of impurities on boiling points

When a solid is dissolved in a liquid, the boiling point is raised. How much the temperature is raised depends on the number of particles of the dissolved substance, so the more concentrated the solution, the higher the temperature needed to produce boiling.

Demonstration: boiling point of water and a salt solution

Water has a boiling point of 100°C at normal atmospheric pressure. If common salt (sodium chloride) is added and dissolved, the resulting solution boils at a higher temperature.

In this demonstration some common salt is added to a beaker of distilled water and mixed using a stirring thermometer (①). The beaker is heated using the heat from a Bunsen burner. The temperature of the water is noted during boiling. In this demonstration it was 105.5°C (②). Check that the thermometer is not touching the sides of the beaker when you note the temperature readings.

More salt is added, and the solution is brought back to the boil. Once again, the boiling point shown by the stirring thermometer is recorded.

A graph of boiling point against salt concentration can be plotted if desired.

Remarks

Because the purpose of the demonstration was to note that a salt solution produced a higher boiling point than pure water, there is no point in suspending the thermometer in the vapor, as was done in the demonstration on page 56, because the vapor temperature will be that of steam (100°C).

① Salt Stirring thermometer ②
°C
Bunsen burner is used to heat the beaker containing distilled water and which has been placed on a gauze pad and tripod.

The effect of impurities on melting points

The presence of impurities always lowers the melting point. (See page 52 for a demonstration on finding the melting point of a pure substance.)

Demonstration: melting point of a salt solution

In this demonstration some crushed ice is placed in the bottom of a boiling tube, and a stirring thermometer used to determine its temperature. As the ice is stirred, its melting point is seen to be 0°C (①).

Any surplus water is now poured out, and a known amount of sodium chloride (common salt) added (②). In this demonstration 5g were added. The amount of liquid increases, even though all the water had previously been poured out, showing that the salt has caused the ice to melt by using latent heat of melting. This has caused the temperature of the mixture to fall (③). In this case the thermometer reads −10°C. When the temperature has stabilized, it is recorded. A further 5g of salt are added, and the demonstration repeated. By plotting the temperatures against the weight of salt added, a graph can be created of the effect of salt concentration on the melting point of water.

Remarks

At all concentrations this cooling mixture causes (pure) water vapor from the air to condense and freeze on the outside of the tube.

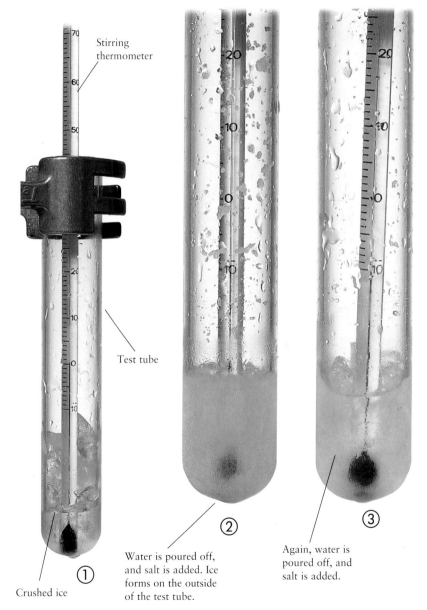

Stirring thermometer

Test tube

① Crushed ice

② Water is poured off, and salt is added. Ice forms on the outside of the test tube.

③ Again, water is poured off, and salt is added.

Changes in boiling point with pressure

The boiling point of a liquid decreases with a decrease in pressure. This apparatus is designed to measure the temperature at which a liquid boils as the pressure is reduced. In the laboratory it is far easier to reduce the pressure below atmospheric than to increase it, which is why this demonstration uses a suction pump.

Demonstration: boiling point changes in ether

The apparatus consists of a side-arm Büchner flask, a pressure gauge, a stirring thermometer, a water-powered suction pump, antibumping granules placed in the bottom of the flask to produce even boiling, and a Petri dish containing water. The liquid being tested for the effects of pressure is ether, which has a relatively low boiling point.

Some ether is poured into the Büchner flask. The flask is sealed with a stopper and stood in the Petri dish, which contains a small amount of water. The purpose of this shallow water bath is to show that heat is not being transferred into the flask during the demonstration and that the changes are therefore due to changes in pressure (i.e., it is a fair test of a single

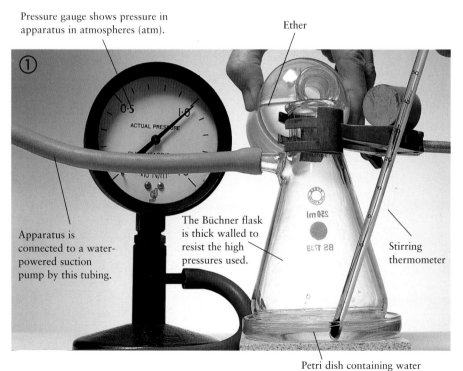

Pressure gauge shows pressure in apparatus in atmospheres (atm).

Ether

Apparatus is connected to a water-powered suction pump by this tubing.

The Büchner flask is thick walled to resist the high pressures used.

Stirring thermometer

Petri dish containing water

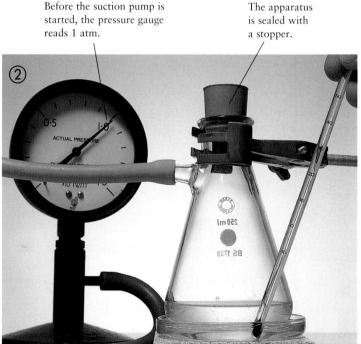

Before the suction pump is started, the pressure gauge reads 1 atm.

The apparatus is sealed with a stopper.

64

variable) (①). The temperature of the water in the Petri dish at the beginning of the demonstration was read off the thermometer as 20°C (②).

The pump is started, and the pressure gauge shows the reduction in pressure. However, the temperature in the water bath, as recorded by the stirring thermometer, hardly changes at all because the thick glass of the flask acts as an insulator for the short time of this demonstration.

When the pressure is reduced to about 0.6 atmospheres (③), the ether begins to boil. Thus merely by reducing the pressure, and without a significant amount of heat being transferred through the walls of the flask, the ether has reached its boiling point.

The suction pump is disconnected immediately so that the apparatus returns to normal pressure. The ether ceases to boil, condensing back to its liquid phase.

(Below) The boiling point temperatures of liquids at low pressure are far below their boiling points at normal pressure. This is why beverages boiled at the top of high mountains only feel warm and, contrastingly, why food cooked in a pressure cooker (where the water temperature reaches 110°C because of the increased pressure maintained inside the vessel) cooks much faster than at atmospheric pressure (there is a halving of cooking time for each 10°C rise in temperature).

EFFECT OF PRESSURE ON THE BOILING POINT OF WATER

Pressure (kPa)	Boiling point of water (°C)
47	80
68	90
100	100
140	110
195	120

NOTE: PASCALS (Pa) are the units used to measure pressure. 100 kilopascals (kPa) is now taken as the standard atmospheric pressure. 1 atm is equivalent to 101,325 Pa is equivalent to 101.325 kPa.

MASTER GLOSSARY

absolute zero: the lowest possible temperature (−273.15°C).

absorption: the process by which a substance is soaked up. *See:* adsorption.

acid: a substance that can give a proton to another substance. Acids are compounds containing hydrogen that can attack and dissolve many substances. Acids are described as weak or strong, dilute or concentrated, mineral or organic. *Example:* hydrochloric acid (HCl). An acid in water can react with a base to form a salt and water.

acidic solution: a solution with a pH lower than 7. *See:* pH.

acidity: a general term for the strength of an acid in a solution.

acid radical: the negative ion left behind when an acid loses a hydrogen ion. *Example:* Cl⁻ in hydrochloric acid (HCl).

acid salt: An ACID SALT contains at least one hydrogen ion and can behave as an acid in chemical reactions. Acid salts are produced under conditions that do not allow complete neutralization of the acid. For example, sulfuric acid may react with a sodium compound to produce a normal sodium salt, sodium sulfate (Na_2SO_4), or it may retain some of the hydrogen, in which case it becomes the salt sodium hydrogen sulfate ($NaHSO_4$).

actinide series or actinide metals: a series of 15 similar radioactive elements between actinium and lawrencium. They are transition metals.

activated charcoal: a form of carbon made of tiny crystals of graphite that is made by heating organic matter in the absence of air. It is then further processed to increase its pore space and therefore its surface area. Its surface area is about 2000 m^2/g. Activated charcoal readily adsorbs many gases, and it is therefore widely used as a filter, for example, in gas masks.

activation energy: the energy required to make a reaction occur. The greater the activation energy of a reaction, the more its reaction rate depends on temperature. The activation energy of a reaction is useful because, if the rate of reaction is known at one temperature (for example, 100 °C) then the activation energy can be used to calculate the rate of reaction at another temperature (for example, at 400 °C) without actually doing the experiment.

adsorption: the process by which a surface adsorbs a substance. The substances involved are not chemically combined and can be separated. *See:* absorption.

alchemy: the traditional "art" of working with chemicals common in the Middle Ages. One of the main challenges for alchemists was to make gold from lead. Alchemy faded away as scientific chemistry was developed in the 17th century.

alcohol: an organic compound that contains a hydroxyl (OH) group. *Example:* ethanol (CH_3CH_2OH), also known as ethyl alcohol or grain alcohol.

alkali/alkaline: a base in (aqueous) solution. Alkalis react with or neutralize hydrogen ions in acids and have a pH greater than 7.0 because they contain relatively few hydrogen ions. *Example:* aqueous sodium hydroxide (NaOH). *See:* pH.

alkaline cell (or battery): a dry cell in which the electrolyte contains sodium or potassium hydroxide.

alkaline earth metal: a member of Group 2 of the Periodic Table. *Example:* calcium.

alkali metals: a member of Group 1 of the Periodic Table. *Example:* sodium.

alkane: a hydrocarbon with no carbon-to-carbon multiple bonds. *Example:* ethane, C_2H_6.

alkene: a hydrocarbon with at least one carbon-to-carbon double bond. *Example:* ethylene, C_2H_4.

alkyne: a hydrocarbon with at least one carbon-to-carbon triple bond. *Example:* acetylene, C_2H_2.

allotropes: alternative forms of an element that differ in the way the atoms are linked. *Example:* white and red phosphorus.

alloy: a mixture of a metal and various other elements. *Example:* brass is an alloy of copper and zinc.

amalgam: a liquid alloy of mercury with another metal.

amorphous: a solid in which the atoms are not arranged regularly (i.e., "glassy"). Compare crystalline.

amphoteric: a metal that will react with both acids and alkalis. *Example:* aluminum metal.

anhydrous: lacking water; water has been removed, for example by heating. (Opposite of anhydrous is hydrous or hydrated.) *Example:* copper(II) sulfate can be anhydrous ($CuSO_4$) or hydrated ($CuSO_4•5H_2O$).

anion: a negatively charged atom or group of atoms. *Examples:* chloride ion (Cl⁻), hydroxide ion (OH⁻).

anode: the electrode at which oxidation occurs; the negative terminal of a battery or the positive electrode of an electrolysis cell.

anodizing: a process that uses the effect of electrolysis to make a surface corrosion-resistant. *Example:* anodized aluminum.

antacid: a common name for any compound that reacts with stomach acid to neutralize it. *Example:* sodium hydrogen carbonate, also known as sodium bicarbonate.

antioxidant: a substance that reacts rapidly with radicals, thereby preventing oxidation of some other substance.

antibumping granules: small glass or ceramic beads designed to promote boiling without the development of large gas bubbles.

approximate relative atomic mass: *See:* relative atomic mass.

aqueous: a solution in which the solvent is water. Usually used as "aqueous solution." *Example:* aqueous solution of sodium hydroxide (NaOH(aq)).

aromatic hydrocarbons: compounds of carbon that have the benzene ring as part of their structure. *Examples:* benzene (C_6H_6), naphthalene ($C_{10}H_8$). They are known as aromatic because of their strong pungent smell.

atmospheric pressure: the pressure exerted by the gases in the air. Units of measurement are kilopascals (kPa), atmospheres (atm), millimeters of mercury (mm Hg), and Torr. Standard atmospheric pressure is 100 kPa, 1atm, 760 mm Hg or 760 Torr.

atom: the smallest particle of an element; a nucleus and its surrounding electrons.

atomic mass: the mass of an atom measured in atomic mass units (u). An atomic mass unit equals one twelfth of the atom of carbon-12.

"Atomic mass" is now more generally used than "atomic weight." *Example:* the atomic mass of chlorine is about 35 u. *See:* atomic weight, relative atomic mass.

atomic number: also known as proton number. The number of electrons or the number of protons in an atom. *Example:* the atomic number of gold is 79.

atomic structure: the nucleus and the arrangement of electrons around it.

atomic weight: a common term used to mean the average molar mass of an element (g/mol). This is the mass per mole of atoms. *Example:* the atomic weight of chlorine is about 35 g/mol. *See:* atomic mass, mole.

base: a substance that can accept a proton from another substance. *Example:* aqueous ammonia ($NH_3(aq)$). A base can react with an acid in water to form a salt and water.

basic salt: a salt that contains at least one hydroxide ion. The hydroxide ion can then behave as a base in chemical reactions. *Example:* the reaction of hydrochloric acid (HCl) with the base aluminum hydroxide ($Al(OH)_3$) can form two basic salts, $Al(OH)_2Cl$ and $Al(OH)Cl_2$.

battery: a number of electrochemical cells placed in series.

bauxite: a hydrated impure oxide of aluminum ($Al_2O_3•xH_2O$, with the amount of water x being variable). It is the main ore used to obtain aluminum metal. The reddish brown color of bauxite is mainly caused by the iron oxide impurities it contains.

beehive shelf: an inverted earthenware bowl with a hole in the upper surface and a slot in the rim. Traditionally the earthenware was brown and looked similar to a beehive, hence its name. A delivery tube passes through the slot, and a gas jar is placed over the hole. This provides a convenient way to collect gas over water in a pneumatic trough.

bell jar: a tall glass jar with an open bottom and a wide, stoppered neck that is used in conjunction with a beehive shelf and a pneumatic trough in some experiments involving gases. The name derives from historic versions of the apparatus, which resembled a bell in shape.

blast furnace: a tall furnace charged with a mixture of iron ore, coke, and limestone and used for the refining of iron metal. The name comes from the strong blast of air introduced during smelting.

bleach: a substance that removes color from stains on materials either by oxidizing or reducing the staining compound. *Example:* sulfur dioxide (SO_2).

block: one of the main divisions of the Periodic Table. Blocks are named for the outermost occupied electron shell of an element. *Example:* the Transition Metals all belong to the d-block.

boiling point: the temperature at which a liquid boils, changing from a liquid to a gas. Boiling points change with atmospheric pressure. *Example:* The boiling point of pure water at standard atmospheric pressure is 100 °C.

boiling tube: A thin glass tube closed at one end and used for chemical tests. The composition and thickness of the glass is such that it cannot sustain very high temperatures and is intended for heating liquids to boiling point. *See:* side-arm boiling tube, test tube.

bond: chemical bonding is either a transfer or sharing of electrons by two or more atoms. There are a number of types of chemical bond, some very strong (such as covalent and ionic bonds), others weak (such as hydrogen bonds). Chemical bonds form because the linked molecule is more stable than the unlinked atoms from which it formed. *Example:* the hydrogen molecule (H_2) is more stable than single atoms of hydrogen, which is why hydrogen gas is always found as molecules of two hydrogen atoms.

Boyle's Law: At constant temperature, and for a given mass of gas, the volume of the gas (V) is inversely proportional to pressure that builds up (P): $P \propto 1/V$.

brine: a solution of salt (sodium chloride, NaCl) in water.

Büchner flask: a thick-walled side-arm flask designed to withstand the changes in pressure that occur when the flask is connected to a suction pump.

Büchner funnel: a special design of plastic or ceramic funnel that has a flat stage on which a filter paper can be placed. It is intended for use under suction with a Büchner funnel.

buffer (solution): a mixture of substances in solution that resists a change in the acidity or alkalinity of the solution when small amounts of an acid or alkali are added.

burette: a long, graduated glass tube with a tap at one end. A burette is used vertically, with the tap lowermost, as a reservoir for a chemical during titration.

burn: a combustion reaction in which a flame is produced. A flame occurs where *gases* combust and release heat and light. At least two gases are therefore required if there is to be a flame. *Example:* methane gas (CH_4) burns in oxygen gas (O_2) to produce carbon dioxide (CO_2) and water (H_2O) and give out heat and light.

calorimeter: an insulated container designed to prevent heat gain or loss with the environment and thus allow changes of temperature within reacting chemicals to be measured accurately. It is named after the old unit of heat, the calorie.

capillary: a very small diameter (glass) tube. Capillary tubing has a small enough diameter to allow surface tension effects to retain water within the tube.

capillary action: the tendency for a liquid to be sucked into small spaces, such as between objects and through narrow-pore tubes. The force to do this comes from surface tension.

carbohydrate: a compound containing only carbon, hydrogen and oxygen. Carbohydrates have the formula $C_n(H_2O)_n$, where n is variable. *Example:* glucose ($C_6H_{12}O_6$).

carbonate: a salt of carbonic acid. Carbonate ions have the chemical formula CO_3^{2-}. *Examples:* calcium nitrate $CaCO_3$ and sodium carbonate Na_2CO_3.

catalyst: a substance that speeds up a chemical reaction but itself remains unaltered at the end of the reaction. *Example:* copper in the reaction of hydrochloric acid with zinc.

catalytic converter: a device incorporated into some exhaust systems. The catalytic converter contains a framework or granules with a very large surface area and coated with catalysts that convert the pollutant gases passing over them into harmless products.

cathode: the electrode at which reduction occurs; the positive terminal of a battery or the negative electrode of an electrolysis cell.

cathodic protection: the technique of protecting a metal object by connecting it to a more readily oxidizable metal. The metal object being protected is made into the cathode of a cell. *Example:* iron can be protected by coupling it with magnesium. Iron forms the cathode and magnesium the anode.

cation: a positively charged ion. *Examples:* calcium ion (Ca^{2+}), ammonium ion (NH_4^+).

caustic: a substance that can cause burns if it touches the skin. *Example:* Sodium hydroxide, caustic soda (NaOH).

Celsius scale (°C): a temperature scale on which the freezing point of water is at 0 degrees, and the normal boiling point at standard atmospheric pressure is 100 degrees.

cell: a vessel containing two electrodes and an electrolyte that can act as an electrical conductor.

centrifuge: an instrument for spinning small samples very rapidly. The fast spin makes the components of a mixture that have a different density separate, as in filtration.

ceramic: a material based on clay minerals that has been heated so that it has chemically hardened.

chalcogens: the members of Group 6 of the Periodic Table: oxygen, sulfur, selenium and tellurium. The word comes from the Greek meaning "brass giver," because all these elements are found in copper ores, and copper is the most important metal in making brass.

change of state: a change between two of the three states of matter, solid, liquid, and gas. *Example:* when water evaporates it changes from a liquid to a gaseous state.

Charles's Law: The volume (V) of a given mass of gas at constant pressure is directly proportional to its absolute temperature (T): $V \propto T$.

chromatography: A separation technique uses the ability of

surfaces to adsorb substances with different strengths. The substances with the least adherence to the surface move faster and leave behind those that adhere more strongly.

coagulation: a term describing the tendency of small particles to stick together in clumps.

coherent: meaning that a substance holds together or sticks together well, and without holes or other defects. *Example:* Aluminum appears unreactive because, as soon as new metal is exposed to air, it forms a very complete oxide coating, which then stops further reaction occurring.

coinage metals: the elements copper, silver, and gold, used to make coins.

coke: a solid substance left after the gases have been extracted from coal.

colloid: a mixture of ultramicroscopic particles dispersed uniformly through a second substance to form a suspension that may be almost like a solution or may set to a jelly (gel). The word comes from the Greek for glue.

colorimeter: an instrument for measuring the light-absorbing power of a substance. The absorption gives an accurate indication of the concentration of some colored solutions.

combustion: a reaction in which an element or compound is oxidized to release energy. Some combustion reactions are slow, such as the combustion of the sugar we eat to provide energy. If the combustion results in a flame, it is called burning. A flame occurs where *gases* combust and release heat and light. At least two gases are therefore required if there is to be a flame. *Example:* the combustion or burning of methane gas (CH_4) in oxygen gas (O_2) produces carbon dioxide (CO_2)

and water (H_2O) and gives out heat and light. Some combustion reactions produce light and heat but do not produce flames. *Example:* the combustion of carbon in oxygen produces an intense red-white light but no flame.

combustion spoon: also known as a deflagrating spoon, it consists of a long metal handle with a small cup at the end. Its purpose is to allow the safe introduction of a (usually heated) substance into a filled gas jar, when the reaction is likely to be vigorous. *Example:* the introduction of a heated sodium pellet into a gas jar containing chlorine.

compound: a chemical consisting of two or more elements chemically bonded together. *Example:* Calcium atoms can combine with carbon atoms and oxygen atoms to make calcium carbonate ($CaCO_3$), a compound of all three atoms.

condensation: the formation of a liquid from a gas. This is a change of state, also called a phase change.

condensation nuclei: microscopic particles of dust, salt, and other materials suspended in the air that attract water molecules. The usual result is the formation of water droplets.

condensation polymer: a polymer formed by a chain of reactions in which a water molecule is eliminated as every link of the polymer is formed. *Examples:* polyesters, proteins, nylon.

conduction: (i) the exchange of heat (heat conduction) by contact with another object, or (ii) allowing the flow of electrons (electrical conduction).

conductivity: the ability of a substance to conduct. The conductivity of a solution depends on there being suitable free ions in the solution. A conducting solution is called an electrolyte. *Example:* dilute sulfuric acid.

convection: the exchange of heat energy with the surroundings produced by the flow of a fluid due to being heated or cooled.

corrosion: the oxidation of a metal. Corrosion is often regarded as unwanted and is more generally used to refer to the *slow* decay of a metal resulting from contact with gases and liquids in the environment. *Example:* Rust is the corrosion of iron.

corrosive: causing corrosion. *Example:* Sodium hydroxide (NaOH).

covalent bond: this is the most common form of strong chemical bonding and occurs when two atoms *share* electrons. *Example:* oxygen (O_2)

cracking: breaking down complex molecules into simpler compounds, as in oil refining.

crucible: a small bowl with a lip, made of heat-resistant white glazed ceramic. It is used for heating substances using a Bunsen flame.

crude oil: a chemical mixture of petroleum liquids. Crude oil forms the raw material for an oil refinery.

crystal: a substance that has grown freely so that it can develop external faces. Compare with crystalline, where the atoms are not free to form individual crystals, and amorphous, where the atoms are arranged irregularly.

crystalline: a solid in which the atoms, ions, or molecules are organized into an orderly pattern without distinct crystal faces. *Examples:* copper(II) sulfate, sodium chloride. Compare amorphous.

crystallization: the process in which a solute comes out of solution slowly and forms crystals. *See:* water of crystallization.

crystal systems: seven patterns or systems into which all crystals can be grouped: cubic, hexagonal, rhombohedral, tetragonal, orthorhombic, monoclinic, and triclinic.

cubic crystal system: groupings of crystals that look like cubes.

current: an electric current is produced by a flow of electrons through a conducting solid or ions through a conducting liquid. The rate of supply of this charge is measured in amperes (A).

decay (radioactive decay): the way that a radioactive element changes into another element due to loss of mass through radiation. *Example:* uranium 238 decays with the loss of an alpha particle to form thorium 234.

decomposition: the break down of a substance (for example, by heat or with the aid of a catalyst) into simpler components. In such a chemical reaction only one substance is involved. *Example:* hydrogen peroxide ($H_2O_2(aq)$) into oxygen ($O_2(g)$) and water ($H_2O(l)$).

decrepitation: when, as part of the decomposition of a substance, cracking sounds are also produced. *Example:* heating of lead nitrate ($Pb(NO_3)_2$).

dehydration: the removal of water from a substance by heating it, placing it in a dry atmosphere, or using a drying (dehydrating) reagent such as concentrated sulfuric acid.

density: the mass per unit volume (e.g., g/cc).

desalinization: the removal of all the salts from sea water, by reverse osmosis or heating the water and collecting the distillate. It is a very energy-intensive process.

desiccant: a substance that absorbs water vapor from the air. *Example:* silica gel.

desiccator: a lidded glass bowl containing a shelf. The apparatus is designed to store materials in dry air. A desiccant is placed below the shelf, and the substance to be dried is placed on the shelf. The lid makes a gas-tight joint with the bowl.

destructive distillation: the heating of a material so that it decomposes entirely to release all of its volatile components. Destructive distillation is also known as pyrolysis.

detergent: a chemical based on petroleum that removes dirt.

Devarda's alloy: zinc with a trace of copper that acts as a catalyst for reactions with the zinc.

diaphragm: a semipermeable membrane – a kind of ultrafine mesh filter – that allows only small ions to pass through. It is used in the electrolysis of brine.

diffusion: the slow mixing of one substance with another until the two substances are evenly mixed. Mixing occurs because of differences in concentration within the mixture. Diffusion works rapidly with gases, very slowly with liquids.

diffusion combustion: the form of combustion that occurs when two gases just begin to mix during ignition. As a result, the flame is hollow and yellow in color. *Example:* a candle flame.

dilute acid: an acid whose concentration has been reduced in a large proportion of water.

disinfectant: a chemical that kills bacteria and other microorganisms.

displacement reaction: a reaction that occurs because metals differ in their reactivity. If a more reactive metal is placed in a solution of a less reactive metal compound, a reaction occurs in which the more reactive metal displaces the metal ions in the solution. *Example:* when zinc metal is introduced into a solution of copper(II) sulfate (which thus contains copper ions), zinc goes into solution as zinc ions, while copper is displaced from the solution and forced to precipitate as metallic copper.

dissociate: to break bonds apart. In the case of acids it means to break up forming hydrogen ions. This is an example of ionization. Strong acids dissociate completely. Weak acids are not completely ionized, and a solution of a weak acid has a relatively low concentration of hydrogen ions.

dissolve: to break down a substance in a solution without causing a reaction.

distillation: the process of separating mixtures by condensing the vapors through cooling.

distilled water: distilled water is nearly pure water and is produced by distillation of tap water. Distilled water is used in the laboratory in preference to tap water because the distillation process removes many of the impurities in tap water that may influence the chemical reactions for which the water is used.

Dreschel bottle: a tall bottle with a special stopper designed to allow a gas to pass through a liquid. The stopper contains both inlet and outlet tubes. One tube extends below the surface of the liquid so that the gas has to pass through the liquid before it can escape to the outlet tube.

dropper funnel: a special funnel with a tap to allow the controlled release of a liquid. Also known as a dropping funnel or tap funnel.

drying agent: *See:* dehydrating agent.

dye: a colored substance that will stick to another substance so that both appear colored.

effervesce: to give off bubbles of gas.

effloresce: to lose water and turn to a fine powder on exposure to the air. *Example:* Sodium carbonate on the rim of a reagent bottle stopper.

electrical conductivity: *See:* conductivity

electrical potential: the energy produced by an electrochemical cell and measured by the voltage or electromotive force (emf). *See:* potential difference, electromotive force.

electrochemical cell: a cell consisting of two electrodes and an electrolyte. It can be set up to generate an electric current (usually known as a galvanic cell, an example of which is a battery), or an electric current can be passed through it to produce a chemical reaction (in which case it is called an electrolytic cell and can be used to refine metals or for electroplating).

electrochemical series: the arrangement of substances that are either oxidizing or reducing agents in order of strength as a reagent, for example, with the strong oxidizing agents at the top of the list and the strong reducing agents at the bottom.

electrode: a conductor that forms one terminal of a cell.

electrolysis: an electrical-chemical process that uses an electric current to cause the breakup of a compound and the movement of metal ions in a solution. The process happens in many natural situations (as for example in rusting) and is also commonly used in industry for purifying (refining) metals or for plating metal objects with a fine, even metal coating.

electrolyte: an ionic solution that conducts electricity.

electrolytic cell: *See:* electrochemical cell

electromotive force (emf): the force set up in an electric circuit by a potential difference.

electron: a tiny, negatively charged particle that is part of an atom. The flow of electrons through a solid material such as a wire produces an electric current.

electron configuration: the pattern in which electrons are arranged in shells around the nucleus of an atom. *Example:* chlorine has the configuration 2, 8, 7.

electroplating: depositing a thin layer of a metal onto the surface of another substance using electrolysis.

element: a substance that cannot be decomposed into simpler substance by chemical means. *Examples:* calcium, iron, gold.

emulsion: tiny droplets of one substance dispersed in another. One common oil in water emulsion is called milk. Because the tiny droplets tend to come together, another stabilizing substance is often needed. Soaps and detergents are such agents, wrapping the particles of grease and oil in a stable coat. Photographic film is an example of a solid emulsion.

endothermic reaction: a reaction that takes in heat. *Example:* when ammonium chloride is dissolved in water.

end point: the stage in a titration when the reaction between the titrant (added from a burette) and the titrate (in the flask) is complete. The end point is normally recognized by use of an indicator that has been added to the titrate. In an acid-base reaction this is also called the neutralization point.

enzyme: biological catalysts in the form of proteins in the body that speed up chemical reactions. Every living cell contains hundreds of enzymes that help the processes of life continue.

ester: organic compounds formed by the reaction of an alcohol with an acid and which often have a fruity taste. *Example:* ethyl acetate ($CH_3COOC_2H_5$).

evaporation: the change of state of a liquid to a gas. Evaporation happens below the boiling point and is used as a method of separating the materials in a solution.

excess, to: if a reactant has been added to another reactant in excess, it has exceeded the amount required to complete the reaction.

exothermic reaction: a reaction that gives out substantial amounts of heat. *Example:* sucrose and concentrated sulfuric acid.

explosive: a substance that, when a shock is applied to it, decomposes very rapidly, releasing a very large amount of heat and creating a large volume of gases as a shock wave.

fat: semisolid, energy-rich compounds derived from plants or animals, made of carbon, hydrogen, and oxygen.

ferment: to break down a substance by microorganisms in the absence of oxygen. *Example:* fermentation of sugar to ethyl alcohol during the production of alcoholic drinks.

filtrate: the liquid that has passed through a filter.

filtration: the separation of a liquid from a solid using a membrane with small holes (i.e. a filter paper).

flame: a mixture of gases undergoing burning. A solid or liquid must produce a gas before it can react with oxygen and burn with a flame.

flammable (also inflammable): able to burn (in air). *Opposite:* nonflammable.

flocculation: the grouping together of small particles in a suspension to form particles large enough to settle out as a precipitate. Flocculation is usually caused by the presence of a flocculating agent. *Example:* calcium ions are the flocculating agent for suspended clay particles.

fluid: able to flow; either a liquid or a gas.

fluorescent: a substance that gives out visible light when struck by invisible waves, such as ultraviolet rays.

flux: a material used to make it easier for a liquid to flow. A flux dissolves metal oxides and so prevents a metal from oxidizing while being heated.

foam: a substance that is sufficiently gelatinous to be able to contain bubbles of gas. The gas bulks up the substance, making it behave as though it were semirigid.

fossil fuels: hydrocarbon compounds that have been formed from buried plant and animal remains. High pressures and temperatures lasting over millions of years are required. *Examples:* The fossil fuels are coal, oil and natural gas.

fraction: a group of similar components of a mixture. *Example:* In the petroleum industry the light fractions of crude oil are those with the smallest molecules, while the medium and heavy fractions have larger molecules.

fractional distillation: the separation of the components of a liquid mixture by heating them to their boiling points.

fractionating column: a glass column designed to allow different fractions to be separated when they boil. In industry it may be called a fractionating tower.

free radical: a very reactive atom or group with a "spare" electron. *Example:* methyl, $CH_3\bullet$.

freezing point: the temperature at which a substance undergoes a phase change from a liquid to a solid. It is the same temperature as the melting point.

fuel: a concentrated form of chemical energy. The main sources of fuels (called fossil fuels because they were formed by geological processes) are coal, crude oil, and natural gas.

fuel rods: the rods of uranium or other radioactive material used as a fuel in nuclear power plants.

fume chamber or fume cupboard: a special laboratory chamber fitted with a protective glass shield and containing a powerful extraction fan to remove toxic fumes.

fuming: an unstable liquid that gives off a gas. Very concentrated acid solutions are often fuming solutions. *Example:* fuming nitric acid.

galvanizing: applying a thin zinc coating to protect another metal.

gamma rays: waves of radiation produced as the nucleus of a radioactive element rearranges itself into a tighter cluster of protons and neutrons. Gamma rays carry enough energy to damage living cells.

gangue: the unwanted material in an ore.

gas/gaseous phase: a form of matter in which the molecules form no definite shape and are free to move about to uniformly fill any vessel they are put in. A gas can easily be compressed into a much smaller volume.

gas syringe: a glass syringe with a graduated cylinder designed to collect and measure small amounts of gases produced during an experiment.

gelatinous precipitate: a precipitate that has a jelly-like appearance. *Example:* iron (III) hydroxide. Because a gelatinous precipitate is mostly water, it is of a similar density to water and will float or lie suspended in the liquid. *See:* granular precipitate.

glass: a transparent silicate without any crystal growth. It has a glassy luster and breaks with a curved fracture. Note that some minerals have all these features and are therefore natural glasses. Household glass is a synthetic silicate.

glucose: the most common of the natural sugars ($C_6H_{12}O_6$). It occurs as the polymer known as cellulose, the fiber in plants. Starch is also a form of glucose.

granular precipitate: a precipitate that has a grainlike appearance. *Example:* lead(II) hydroxide. *See:* gelatinous precipitate.

gravimetric analysis: a quantitative form of analysis in which the mass (weight) of the reactants and products is measured.

group: a vertical column in the Periodic Table. There are eight groups in the table. Their numbers correspond to the number of electrons in the outer shell of the atoms in the group. *Example:* Group 1: member, sodium.

Greenhouse Effect: an increase in the global air temperature as a result of heat released from burning fossil fuels being absorbed by carbon dioxide in the atmosphere.

Greenhouse gas: any of various gases that contribute to the Greenhouse Effect. *Example:* carbon dioxide.

half-life: the time it takes for the radiation coming from a sample of a radioactive element to decrease by half.

halide: a salt of one of the halogens.

halogen: one of a group of elements including chlorine, bromine, iodine, and fluorine in Group 7 of the Periodic Table.

heat: the energy that is transferred when a substance is at a different temperature than its surroundings. *See:* endothermic and exothermic reactions.

heat capacity: the ratio of the heat supplied to a substance compared to the rise in temperature that is produced.

heat of combustion: the amount of heat given off by a mole of a substance during combustion. This heat is a property of the substance and is the same no matter what kind of combustion is involved. *Example:* heat of combustion of carbon is 94.05 kcal (x 4.18 = 393.1 kJ).

hydrate: a solid compound in crystalline form that contains water molecules. Hydrates commonly form when a solution of a soluble salt is evaporated. The water that forms part of a hydrate crystal is known as the "water of crystallization." It can usually be removed by heating, leaving an anhydrous salt.

hydration: the process of absorption of water by a substance. In some cases hydration makes the substance change color; in many other cases there is no color change, simply a change in volume. *Example:* dark blue hydrated copper(II) sulfate ($CuSO_4 \cdot 5H_2O$) can be heated to produce white anhydrous copper(II) sulfate ($CuSO_4$).

hydride: a compound containing just hydrogen and another element, most often a metal. *Examples:* water (H_2O), methane (CH_4) and phosphine (PH_3).

hydrous: hydrated with water. *See:* anhydrous.

hydrocarbon: a compound in which only hydrogen and carbon atoms are present. Most fuels are hydrocarbons, as is the simple plastic polyethylene. *Example:* methane CH_4.

hydrogen bond: a type of attractive force that holds one molecule to another. It is one of the weaker forms of intermolecular attractive force. *Example:* hydrogen bonds occur in water.

ignition temperature: the temperature at which a substance begins to burn.

immiscible: will not mix with another substance. e.g., oil and water.

incandescent: glowing or shining with heat. *Example:* tungsten filament in an incandescent light bulb.

incomplete combustion: combustion in which only some of the reactant or reactants combust, or the products are not those that would be obtained if all the reactions went to completion. It is uncommon for combustion to be complete, and incomplete combustion is more frequent. *Example:* incomplete combustion of carbon in oxygen produces carbon monoxide and not carbon dioxide.

indicator (acid-base indicator): a substance or mixture of substances used to test the acidity or alkalinity of a substance. An indicator changes color depending on the acidity of the solution being tested. Many indicators are complicated organic substances. Some indicators used in the laboratory include Universal Indicator, litmus, phenolphthalein, methyl orange and bromothymol. *See:* Universal Indicator.

induction period: the time taken for a reaction to reach ignition temperature. During this period no apparent reaction occurs; then the materials appear to undergo spontaneous combustion.

inert: unreactive.

inhibitor: a substance that prevents a reaction from occurring.

inorganic substance: a substance that does not contain carbon and hydrogen. Examples: NaCl, $CaCO_3$.

insoluble: a substance that will not dissolve.

ion: an atom, or group of atoms, that has gained or lost one or more electrons and so developed an electrical charge. Ions behave differently than electrically neutral atoms and molecules. They can move in an electric field, and they can also bind strongly to solvent molecules such as water. Positively charged ions are called cations; negatively charged ions are called anions. Ions can carry an electrical current through solutions.

ionic bond: the form of bonding that occurs between two ions when the ions have opposite charges. *Example:* sodium cations bond with chloride anions to form common salt (NaCl) when a salty solution is evaporated. Ionic bonds are strong bonds except in the presence of a solvent. *See:* bond.

ionic compound: a compound that consists of ions. *Example:* NaCl.

ionize: to break up neutral molecules into oppositely charged ions or to convert atoms into ions by the loss of electrons.

ionization: a process that creates ions.

isotope: an atom that has the same number of protons in its nucleus, but which has a different mass. *Example:* carbon 12 and carbon 14.

Kipp's apparatus: a piece of glassware consisting of three chambers, designed to provide a continuous and regulated production of gas by bringing the reactants into contact in a controlled way.

lanthanide series or lanthanide metals: a series of 15 similar metallic elements between lanthanum and lutetium. They are transition metals and are also called rare earths.

latent heat: the amount of heat that is absorbed or released during the process of changing state between gas, liquid, or solid. For example, heat is absorbed when a substance melts, and it is released again when the substance solidifies.

lattice: a regular arrangement of atoms, ions, or molecules in a crystalline solid.

leaching: the extraction of a substance by percolating a solvent through a material. *Example:* when water flows through an ore, some of the heavy metals in it may be leached out causing environmental pollution.

Liebig condenser: a piece of glassware consisting of a sloping, water-cooled tube. The design allows a volatile material to be condensed and collected.

liquefaction: to make something liquid.

liquid/liquid phase: a form of matter that has a fixed volume but no fixed shape.

lime (quicklime): calcium oxide (CaO). A white, caustic solid manufactured by heating limestone and used for making mortar, fertilizer, or bleach.

limewater: an aqueous solution of calcium hydroxide used especially to detect the presence of carbon dioxide.

litmus: an indicator obtained from lichens. Used as a solution or impregnated into paper (litmus paper) that is dampened before use. Litmus turns red under acid conditions and purple in alkaline conditions. Litmus is a crude indicator when compared with Universal Indicator.

load (electronics): an impedance or circuit that receives or develops the output of a cell or other power supply.

luster: the shininess of a substance.

malleable: able to be pressed or hammered into shape.

manometer: a device for measuring gas pressure. A simple manometer is made by partly filling a U-shaped rubber tube with water and connecting one end to the source of gas whose pressure is to be measured. The pressure is always relative to atmospheric pressure.

mass: the amount of matter in an object. In everyday use the word weight is often used (somewhat incorrectly) to mean mass.

matter: anything that has mass and takes up space.

melting point: the temperature at which a substance changes state from a solid phase to a liquid phase. It is the same as freezing point.

membrane: a thin flexible sheet. A semipermeable membrane has microscopic holes of a size that will selectively allow some ions and molecules to pass through but hold others back. It thus acts as a kind of filter. *Example:* a membrane used for osmosis.

meniscus: the curved surface of a liquid that forms in a small-bore or capillary tube. The meniscus is convex (bulges upward) for mercury and is concave (sags downward) for water.

metal: a class of elements that is a good conductor of electricity and heat, has a metallic luster, is malleable and ductile, forms cations, and has oxides that are bases. Metals are formed as cations held together by a sea of electrons. A metal may also be an alloy of these elements. *Example:* sodium, calcium, gold. *See:* alloy, metalloid, nonmetal.

metallic bonding: cations reside in a "sea" of mobile electrons. It allows metals to be good conductors and means that they are not brittle. *See:* bonding.

metallic luster: *See:* luster.

metalloid: a class of elements intermediate in properties between metals and nonmetals. Metalloids are also called semimetals or semiconductors. *Example:* silicon, germanium, antimony. *See:* metal, nonmetal, semiconductor.

micronutrient: an element that the body requires in small amounts. Another term is trace element.

mineral: a solid substance made of just one element or compound. *Example:* calcite is a mineral because it consists only of calcium carbonate; halite is a mineral because it contains only sodium chloride.

mineral acid: an acid that does not contain carbon and which attacks minerals. Hydrochloric, sulfuric, and nitric acids are the main mineral acids.

miscible: capable of being mixed.

mixing combustion: the form of combustion that occurs when two gases thoroughly mix before they ignite and so produce almost complete combustion. *Example:* when a Bunsen flame is blue.

mixture: a material that can be separated into two or more substances using physical means. *Example:* a mixture of copper(II) sulfate and cadmium sulfide can be separated by filtration.

molar mass: the mass per mole of atoms of an element. It has the same value and uses the same units as atomic weight. *Example:* molar mass of chlorine is 35.45 g/mol. *See:* atomic weight.

mole: 1 mole is the amount of a substance that contains Avagadro's number (6×10^{23}) of particles. *Example:* 1 mole of carbon-12 weighs exactly 12 g.

molecular mass: *See:* molar mass.

molecular weight: *See:* molar mass.

molecule: a group of two or more atoms held together by chemical bonds. *Example:* O_2.

monoclinic system: a grouping of crystals that look like double-ended chisel blades.

monomer: a small molecule and building block for larger chain molecules or polymers ("mono"

means one, "mer" means part). *Examples:* tetrafluoroethene for teflon, ethene for polyethene.

native element: an element that occurs in an uncombined state. *Examples:* sulfur, gold.

native metal: a pure form of a metal, not combined as a compound. Native metal is more common in poorly reactive elements than in those that are very reactive. *Examples:* copper, gold.

net ionic reaction: the overall, or net, change that occurs in a reaction, seen in terms of ions.

neutralization: the reaction of acids and bases to produce a salt and water. The reaction causes hydrogen from the acid and hydroxide from the base to be changed to water. *Example:* hydrochloric acid reacts with, and neutralizes, sodium hydroxide to form the salt sodium chloride (common salt) and water. The term is more generally used for any reaction in which the pH changes toward 7.0, which is the pH of a neutral solution. *See:* pH.

neutralization point: *See:* end point.

neutron: a particle inside the nucleus of an atom that is neutral and has no charge.

newton (N): the unit of force required to give one kilogram an acceleration of one meter per second every second (1 ms^{-2}).

nitrate: a compound that includes nitrogen and oxygen and contains more oxygen than a nitrite. Nitrate ions have the chemical formula NO_3^-. *Examples:* sodium nitrate $NaNO_3$ and lead nitrate $Pb(NO_3)_2$.

nitrite: a compound that includes nitrogen and oxygen and contains less oxygen than a nitrate. Nitrite ions have the chemical formula NO_2^-. *Example:* sodium nitrite $NaNO_2$.

noble gases: the members of Group 8 of the Periodic Table: helium, neon, argon, krypton, xenon, radon. These gases are almost entirely unreactive.

noble metals: silver, gold, platinum, and mercury. These are the least reactive metals.

noncombustible: a substance that will not combust or burn. *Example:* carbon dioxide.

nonmetal: a brittle substance that does not conduct electricity. *Examples:* sulfur, phosphorus, all gases. *See:* metal, metalloid.

normal salt: salts that do not contain a hydroxide (OH^-) ion, which would make them basic salts, or a hydrogen ion, which would make them acid salts. *Example:* sodium chloride ($NaCl$).

nucleus: the small, positively charged particle at the center of an atom. The nucleus is responsible for most of the mass of an atom.

opaque: a substance that will not transmit light so that it is impossible to see through it. Most solids are opaque.

ore: a rock containing enough of a useful substance to make mining it worthwhile. *Example:* bauxite, aluminum ore.

organic acid: an acid containing carbon and hydrogen. *Example:* methanoic (formic) acid ($HCOOH$).

organic chemistry: the study of organic compounds.

organic compound (organic substance; organic material): a compound (or substance) that contains carbon and usually hydrogen. (The carbonates are usually excluded.) *Examples:* methane (CH_4), chloromethane (CH_3Cl), ethene (C_2H_4), ethanol (C_2H_5OH), ethanoic acid (C_2H_3OOH) etc.

organic solvent: an organic substance that will dissolve other substances. *Example:* carbon tetrachloride (CCl_4).

osmosis: a process whereby molecules of a liquid solvent move through a semipermeable membrane from a region of low concentration of a solute to a region with a high concentration of a solute.

oxidation-reduction reaction (redox reaction): reaction in which oxidation and reduction occurs; a reaction in which electrons are transferred. *Example:* copper and oxygen react to produce copper(II) oxide. The copper is oxidized, and oxygen is reduced.

oxidation: combination with oxygen or a reaction in which an atom, ion, or molecule loses electrons to an oxidizing agent. (Note that an oxidizing agent does not have to contain oxygen.) The opposite of oxidation is reduction. *See:* reduction.

oxidation number (oxidation state): the effective charge on an atom in a compound. An increase in oxidation number corresponds to oxidation, and a decrease to reduction. Shown in Roman numerals. *Example:* manganate(IV).

oxidation state: *See:* oxidation number.

oxide: a compound that includes oxygen and one other element. *Example:* copper oxide (CuO).

oxidize: to combine with or gain oxygen or to react such that an atom, ion, or molecule loses electrons to an oxidizing agent.

oxidizing agent: a substance that removes electrons from another substance being oxidized (and therefore is itself reduced) in a redox reaction. *Example:* chlorine (Cl_2).

ozone: a form of oxygen whose molecules contain three atoms of oxygen. Ozone is regarded as a beneficial gas when high in the atmosphere because it blocks ultraviolet rays. It is a harmful gas when breathed in, so low-level ozone that is produced as part of city smog is regarded as a form of pollution. The ozone layer is the uppermost part of the stratosphere.

partial pressure: the pressure a gas in a mixture would exert if it alone occupied a flask. *Example:* oxygen makes up about a fifth of the atmosphere. Its partial pressure is therefore about a fifth of normal atmospheric pressure.

pascal: the unit of pressure, equal to one newton per square meter of surface. *See:* newton.

patina: a surface coating that develops on metals and protects them from further corrosion. *Example:* the green coating on copper carbonate that forms on copper statues.

percolate: to move slowly through the pores of a rock.

period: a row in the Periodic Table.

Periodic Table: a chart organizing elements by atomic number and chemical properties into groups and periods.

pestle and mortar: a pestle is a ceramic rod with a rounded end; a mortar is a ceramic dish. Pestle and mortar are used together to pound or grind solids into fine powders.

Petri dish: a shallow glass or plastic dish with a lid.

petroleum: a natural mixture of a range of gases, liquids, and solids derived from the decomposed remains of plants and animals.

pH: a measure of the hydrogen ion concentration in a liquid. Neutral is pH 7.0; numbers greater than this are alkaline; smaller numbers are acidic. *See:* neutralization, acid, base.

pH meter: a device that accurately measures the pH of a solution. A

pH meter is a voltmeter that measures the electric potential difference between two electrodes (which are attached to the meter through a probe) when they are submerged in a solution. The readings are shown on a dial or digital display.

phase: a particular state of matter. A substance may exist as a solid, liquid, or gas and may change between these phases with addition or removal of energy. *Examples:* ice, liquid, and vapor are the three phases of water. Ice undergoes a phase change to water when heat energy is added.

phosphor: any material that glows when energized by ultraviolet or electron beams such as in fluorescent tubes and cathode ray tubes. Phosphors, such as phosphorus, emit light after the source of excitation is cut off. This is why they glow in the dark. By contrast, fluorescors, such as fluorite, only emit light while they are being excited by ultraviolet light or an electron beam.

photochemical smog: photochemical reactions are caused by the energy of sunlight. Photochemical smog is a mixture of tiny particles and a brown haze caused by the reaction of colorless nitric oxide from vehicle exhausts and oxygen of the air to form brown nitrogen dioxide.

photon: a parcel of light energy.

photosynthesis: the process by which plants use the energy of the Sun to make the compounds they need for life. In photosynthesis six molecules of carbon dioxide from the air combine with six molecules of water, forming one molecule of glucose (sugar) and releasing six molecules of oxygen back into the atmosphere.

pipe-clay triangle: a device made from three small pieces of ceramic tube that are wired together in the shape of a triangle. Pipe-clay

triangles are used to support round-bottomed dishes when they are heated in a Bunsen flame.

pipette: a log, slender glass tube used, in conjunction with a pipette filler, to draw up and then transfer accurately measured amounts of liquid.

plastic: (material) a carbon-based substance consisting of long chains (polymers) of simple molecules. The word plastic is commonly restricted to synthetic polymers. *Examples:* polyvinyl chloride, nylon: **(property)** a material is plastic if it can be made to change shape easily. Plastic materials will remain in the new shape. (Compare with elastic, a property whereby a material goes back to its original shape.)

pneumatic trough: a shallow water-filled glass dish used to house a beehive shelf and a gas jar as part of the apparatus for collecting a gas over water.

polar solvent: a solvent in which the atoms have partial electric charges. *Example:* water.

polymer: a compound that is made of long chains by combining molecules (called monomers) as repeating units. ("Poly" means many, "mer" means part.) *Examples:* polytetrafluoroethene or Teflon from tetrafluoroethene, Terylene from terephthalic acid and ethane-1,2-diol (ethylene glycol).

polymerization: a chemical reaction in which large numbers of similar molecules arrange themselves into large molecules, usually long chains. This process usually happens when there is a suitable catalyst present. *Example:* ethene gas reacts to form polyethene in the presence of certain catalysts.

polymorphism: (meaning many shapes) the tendency of some materials to have more than one solid form. *Example:* carbon as diamond, graphite and buckminsterfullerene.

porous: a material containing many small holes or cracks. Quite often the pores are connected, and liquids, such as water or oil, can move through them.

potential difference: a measure of the work that must be done to move an electric charge from one point to the other in a circuit. Potential difference is measured in volts, V. *See:* electrical potential.

precious metal: silver, gold, platinum, iridium and palladium. Each is prized for its rarity.

precipitate: a solid substance formed as a result of a chemical reaction between two liquids or gases. *Example:* iron (III) hydroxide is precipitated when sodium hydroxide solution is added to iron (III) chloride. *See:* gelatinous precipitate, granular precipitate.

preservative: a substance that prevents the natural organic decay processes from occurring. Many substances can be used safely for this purpose, including sulfites and nitrogen gas.

pressure: the force per unit area measured in pascals. *See:* pascal.

product: a substance produced by a chemical reaction. *Example:* when the reactants copper and oxygen react, they produce the product copper oxide.

proton: a positively charged particle in the nucleus of an atom that balances out the charge of the surrounding electrons.

proton number: this is the modern expression for atomic number. *See:* atomic number.

purify: to remove all impurities from a mixture, perhaps by precipitation or filtration.

pyrolysis: chemical decomposition brought about by heat. *Example:* decomposition of lead nitrate. *See:* destructive distillation.

pyrometallurgy: refining a metal from its ore using heat. A blast furnace or smelter is the main equipment used.

quantitative: measurement of the amounts of constituents of a substance, for example, by mass or volume. *See:* gravimetric analysis, volumetric analysis.

radiation: the exchange of energy with the surroundings through the transmission of waves or particles of energy. Radiation is a form of energy transfer that can happen through space; no intervening medium is required (as would be the case for conduction and convection).

radical: an atom, molecule, or ion with at least one unpaired electron. *Example:* nitrogen monoxide (NO).

radioactive: emitting radiation or particles from the nucleus of its atoms.

radioactive decay: a change in a radioactive element due to loss of mass through radiation. For example, uranium decays (changes) to lead.

reactant: a starting material that takes part in and undergoes change during a chemical reaction. *Example:* hydrochloric acid and calcium carbonate are reactants; the reaction produces the products calcium chloride, carbon dioxide, and water.

reaction: the recombination of two substances using parts of each substance to produce new substances. *Example:* the reactants sodium chloride and sulfuric acid react and recombine to form the products sodium sulfate, chlorine, and water.

reactivity: the tendency of a substance to react with other substances. The term is most widely used in comparing the reactivity of metals. Metals are arranged in a reactivity series.

reactivity series: the series of metals organized in order of their reactivity, with the most reactive metals, such as sodium, at the top and the least react metals, such as gold, at the bottom. Hydrogen is usually included in the series for comparative purposes.

reagent: a commonly available substance (reactant) used to create a reaction. Reagents are the chemicals normally kept on chemistry laboratory shelf. Many substances called reagents are most commonly used for test purposes.

redox reaction (oxidation-reduction reaction): a reaction that involves oxidation and reduction; a reactions in which electrons are transferred. *See:* oxidation-reduction.

reducing agent: a substance that gives electrons to another substance being reduced (and therefore itself being oxidized) in a redox reaction. *Example:* hydrogen sulfide (H_2S).

reduction: the removal of oxygen from, or the addition of hydrogen to, a compound. Also a reaction in which an atom, ion, or molecule gains electrons from a reducing agent. (The opposite of reduction is oxidation.)

reduction tube: a boiling tube with a small hole near the closed end. The tube is mounted horizontally, a sample is placed in the tube, and a reducing gas, such as carbon monoxide, is passed through the tube. The oxidized gas escapes through the small hole.

refining: separating a mixture into the simpler substances of which it is made.

reflux distillation system: a form of distillation using a Liebig condenser placed vertically, so that all the vapors created during boiling are condensed back into the liquid rather than escaping. In this way the concentration of all the reactants remains constant.

relative atomic mass: in the past a measure of the mass of an atom on a scale relative to the mass of an atom of hydrogen, where hydrogen is 1. Nowadays a measure of the mass of an atom relative to the mass of one twelfth of an atom of carbon-12. If the relative atomic mass is given as a rounded figure, it is called an approximate relative atomic mass. *Examples*: chlorine 35, calcium 40, gold 197. *See:* atomic mass, atomic weight.

reversible reaction: a reaction in which the products can be transformed back into their original chemical form. *Example:* heated iron reacts with steam to produce iron oxide and hydrogen. If the hydrogen is passed over this heated oxide it forms iron and steam. $3Fe + 4H_2O \rightleftharpoons Fe_3O_4 + 4H_2$.

roast: heating a substance for a long time at a high temperature, as in a furnace.

rust: the product of the corrosion of iron and steel in the presence of air and water.

salt: a compound, often involving a metal, that is the reaction product of an acid and a base, or of two elements. (Note "salt" is also the common word for sodium chloride, common salt, or table salt.) *Example:* sodium chloride (NaCl) and potassium sulfate (K_2SO_4) *See:* acid salt, basic salt, normal salt.

salt bridge: a permeable material soaked in a salt solution that allows ions to be transferred from one container to another. The salt solution remains unchanged during this transfer. *Example:* sodium sulfate used as a salt bridge in a galvanic cell.

saponification: a reaction between a fat and a base that produces a soap.

saturated: a state in which a liquid can hold no more of a substance. If any more of the substance is added, it will not dissolve.

saturated hydrocarbon: a hydrocarbon in which the carbon atoms are held with single bonds. *Example:* ethane (C_2H_4).

saturated solution: a solution that holds the maximum possible amount of dissolved material. When saturated, the rate of dissolving solid and that of recrystallization solid are the same, and a condition of equilibrium is reached. The amount of material in solution varies with the temperature; cold solutions can hold less dissolved solid material than hot solutions. Gases are more soluble in cold liquids than hot liquids.

sediment: material that settles out at the bottom of a liquid when it is still. A precipitate is one form of sediment.

semiconductor: a material of intermediate conductivity. Semiconductor devices often use silicon when they are made as part of diodes, transistors, or integrated circuits. Elements intermediate between metals and nonmetals are also sometimes called semiconductors. *Example:* germanium oxide, germanium. *See:* metalloid.

semipermeable membrane: a thin material that acts as a fine sieve or filter, allowing small molecules to pass, but holding large molecules back.

separating column: used in chromatography. A tall glass tube containing a porous disc near the base and filled with a substance (for example, aluminum oxide, which is known as a stationary phase) that can adsorb materials on its surface. When a mixture is passed through the column, fractions are retarded by differing amounts, so that each fraction is washed through the column in sequence.

separating funnel: a pear-shaped glassware funnel designed to permit the separation of immiscible liquids by simply pouring off the more dense liquid while leaving the less dense liquid in the funnel.

series circuit: an electrical circuit in which all of the components are joined end to end in a line.

shell: the term used to describe the imaginary ball-shaped surface outside the nucleus of an atom that would be formed by a set of electrons of similar energy. The outermost shell is known as the valence shell. *Example:* neon has shells containing 2 and 8 electrons.

side-arm boiling tube: a boiling tube with an integral glass pipe near its open end. The side arm is normally used for the entry or exit of a gas.

simple distillation: the distillation of a substance when only one volatile fraction is to be collected. Simple distillation uses a Liebig condenser arranged almost horizontally. When the liquid mixture is heated and vapors are produced, they enter the condenser and then flow away from the flask and can be collected. *Example:* simple distillation of ethanoic acid.

slag: a mixture of substances that are waste products of a furnace. Most slags are composed mainly of silicates.

smelting: roasting a substance in order to extract the metal contained in it.

smog: a mixture of smoke and fog. The term is used to describe city fogs in which there is a large proportion of particulate matter (tiny pieces of carbon from exhausts) and also a high concentration of sulfur and nitrogen gases and probably ozone. *See:* photochemical smog.

smokeless fuel: a fuel that has been subjected to partial pyrolysis so that there is no more loose particulate matter remaining. *Example:* Coke is a smokeless fuel.

solid/solid phase: a rigid form of matter that maintains its shape whatever its container.

solubility: the maximum amount of a substance that can be contained in a solvent.

soluble: readily dissolvable in a solvent.

solute: a substance that has dissolved. *Example:* sodium chloride in water.

solution: a mixture of a liquid (the solvent) and at least one other substance of lesser abundance (the solute). Mixtures can be separated by physical means, for example, by evaporation and cooling. *See:* aqueous solution.

solvent: the main substance in a solution.

spectator ions: the ionic part of a compound that does not play an active part in a reaction. *Example:* when magnesium ribbon is placed in copper(II) sulfate solution the copper is displaced from the solution by the magnesium while the sulfate ion (SO_4^{2-}) plays no part in the reaction and so behaves as a spectator ion.

spectrum: the range of colors that make up visible light (as seen in a rainbow) or across all electromagnetic radiation, arranged in progression according to their wavelength.

spontaneous combustion: the effect of a very reactive material or combination of reactants that suddenly reach their ignition temperature and begin to combust rapidly.

standard temperature and pressure (STP): 0°C at one atmosphere (a pressure that supports a column of mercury 760 mm high). Also given as 0°C at 100 kilopascals. *See:* atmospheric pressure.

state of matter: the physical form of matter. There are three states of matter: liquid, solid, and gaseous.

stationary phase: a name given to a material that is used as a medium for separating a liquid mixture, as in in chromatography.

strong acid: an acid that has completely dissociated (ionized) in water. Mineral acids are strong acids.

sublime/sublimation: the change of a substance from solid to gas, or vice versa, without going through a liquid phase. *Example:* iodine sublimes from a purple solid to a purple gas.

substance: a type of material, including mixtures.

sulfate: a compound that includes sulfur and oxygen and contains more oxygen than a sulfite. Sulfate ions have the chemical formula SO_4^{2-}. *Examples:* calcium sulfate $CaSO_4$ (the main constituent of gypsum) and aluminum sulfate $Al_2(SO_4)_3$ (an alum).

sulfide: a sulfur compound that contains no oxygen. Sulfide ions have the chemical formula S^{2-}. *Example:* hydrogen sulfide (H_2S).

sulfite: a compound that includes sulfur and oxygen but contains less oxygen than a sulfate. Sulfite ions have the chemical formula SO_3^{2-}. *Example:* sodium sulfite Na_2SO_3.

supercooling: the ability of some substances to cool below their normal freezing point. *Example:* sodium thiosulfate.

supersaturated solution: a solution in which the amount of solute is greater than what would normally be expected in a saturated solution. Most solids are more soluble in hot solutions than in cold. If a hot saturated solution is made up, the solution can be rapidly cooled down below its freezing point before it begins to solidify. This is a supersaturated solution.

surface tension: the force that operates on the surface of a liquid and that makes it act as though it were covered with an invisible, elastic film.

suspension: a mist of tiny particles in a liquid.

synthesis: a reaction in which a substance is formed from simpler reactants. *Example:* hydrogen gas and chlorine gas react to sythesize hydrogen chloride gas. The term can also be applied to polymerization of organic compounds.

synthetic: does not occur naturally but has to be manufactured. Commonly used in the name "synthetic fiber."

tare: an allowance made for the weight of a container.

tarnish: a coating that develops as a result of the reaction between a metal and substances in the air. The most common form of tarnishing is a very thin transparent oxide coating.

terminal: one of the electrodes of a battery.

test (chemical): a reagent or a procedure used to reveal the presence of another reagent. *Example:* litmus and other indicators are used to test the acidity or alkalinity of a substance.

test tube: A thin glass tube closed at one end and used for chemical tests, etc. The composition and thickness of the glass is such that while it is inert to most chemical reactions, it may not sustain very high temperatures but can usually be heated in a Bunsen flame. *See:* boiling tube.

thermal decomposition: the breakdown of a substance using heat: *See* pyrolysis.

thermoplastic: a plastic that will soften and can repeatedly be molded into shape on heating and will set into the molded shape as it cools.

thermoset: a plastic that will set into a molded shape as it cools, but which cannot be made soft by reheating.

thistle funnel: a narrow tube, expanded at the top into a thistlehead-shaped vessel. It is used as a funnel when introducing small amounts of liquid reactant. When fitted with a tap, it can be used to control the rate of entry of a reactant. *See:* burette.

titration: the analysis of the composition of a substance in a solution by measuring the volume of that solution (the titrant, normally in a burette) needed to react with a given volume of another solution (the titrate, normally placed in a flask). An indicator is often used to signal change. *Example:* neutralization of sodium hydroxide using hydrochloric acid in an acid–base titration. *See:* end point.

toxic: poisonous.

transition metals: the group of metals that belong to the d-block of the Periodic Table. Transition metals commonly have a number of differently colored oxidation states. *Examples:* iron, vanadium.

Universal Indicator: a mixture of indicators commonly used in the laboratory because of its reliability. Used as a solution or impregnated into paper (Indicator paper) that is dampened before use. Universal Indicator changes color from purple in a strongly alkaline solution through green when the solution is neutral to red in strongly acidic solutions. Universal Indicator is more accurate than litmus paper but less accurate than a pH meter.

unsaturated hydrocarbon: a hydrocarbon in which at least one bond is a double or triple bond. Hydrogen atoms can be added to unsaturated compounds to form saturated compounds. *Example:* ethene, C_2H_4 or $CH_2=CH_2$.

vacuum: a container from which air has been removed using a pump.

valency: the number of bonds that an atom can form. *Examples:* calcium has a valency of 2 and bromine a valency of 1

valency shell: the outermost shell of an atom. *See:* shell.

vapor: the gaseous phase of a substance. *See:* gas.

vein: a fissure in rock that has filled with ore or other mineral-bearing rock.

viscous: slow-moving, syrupy. A liquid that has a low viscosity is said to be mobile.

volatile: readily forms a gas.

volatile fraction: the part of a liquid mixture that will readily vaporize under the conditions prevailing during the reaction. *See:* fraction, vapor.

water of crystallization: the water molecules absorbed into the crystalline structure as a liquid changes to a solid. *Example:* hydrated copper(II) sulfate $CuSO_4 \bullet 5H_2O$. *See:* hydrate.

weak acid and **weak base**: an acid or base that has only partly dissociated (ionized) in water. Most organic acids are weak acids. *See:* organic acid.

weight: the gravitational force on a substance. *See:* mass.

X-rays: a form of very short wave radiation.

MASTER INDEX

DATE